THE FORTEAN

Strange Deaths 2

THE **FORTEAN TIMES** BOOK OF
STRANGE DEATHS 2

COMPILED BY
Paul Sieveking

DESIGN & ILLUSTRATIONS
Etienne Gilfillan

COVER ILLUSTRATION
David Newton

EDITOR -IN-CHIEF
David Sutton

PUBLISHING & MARKETING
Paul Rayner
020 7907 6663
paul_rayner@dennis.co.uk

MAGBOOK PUBLISHER
Dharmesh Mistry
020 7907 6100
dharmesh_mistry@dennis.co.uk

MAG BOOK

THE FORTEAN TIMES BOOK OF STRANGE DEATHS is published by Dennis Publishing Ltd, 30 Cleveland Street, London W1T 4JD. Company registered in England. The MagBook brand is a trademark of Dennis Publishing Ltd. All material © Dennis Publishing Ltd, licensed by Felden 2012, and may not be reproduced in any form without the consent of the publishers.
The Fortean Times Book of Strange Deaths 2
ISBN 1-907779-97-3

All material copyright 2012.
Printed at Stones Printers Limited.

LICENSING AND SYNDICATION
To license this product, contact Carlotta Serantoni:
+44 (0)20 7907 6550 / carlotta_serantoni@dennis.co.uk
For syndication enquiries, contact Anj Dosaj Halai:
+44 (0) 20 7907 6132 /anj_dosaj-halai@dennis.co.uk

DENNIS PUBLISHING LTD
Digital Production Manager: Nicky Baker
Operations Director: Robin Ryan
MD of Advertising: Julian Lloyd-Evans
Newstrade Director: David Barker
Commercial & Retail Director: Martin Belson
Chief Operating Officer: Brett Reynolds
Group Finance Director: Ian Leggett

Chief Executive: James Tye
Chairman: Felix Dennis

HOW TO CONTACT US
MAIL: 30 Cleveland Street, London W1T 4JD
PHONE: 020 7907 6000
EMAIL AND WEB
Website: www.forteantimes.com

To contact advertising:
Ciaran Scarry 020 7907 6683
ciaran_scarry@dennis.co.uk

CONTENTS

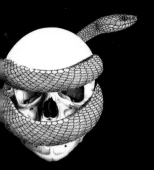

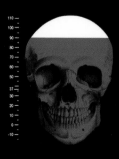

Cosmic Joker

Dying probably never seems like good fortune, but the timing and manner of some departures suggests someone up there is playing a cruel joke...

DON GIACOMO PERINI, A PRIEST, CURSED THE rain as he stood outside his church in Alto Adige, Italy; whereupon a cross, loosened by the rain, fell on his head and killed him. *Sun, 6 Oct 1992.*

BELIEVING THAT HER HUSBAND HAD betrayed her, Vera Czermak of Prague jumped from her third storey window – and landed on him as he passed below. She recovered in hospital, but he died instantly. *D.Record, 28 Nov 1992.*

SALVATORE CHIRILINO PICKED A FOUR-LEAF clover on a clifftop in Vibo Marina, Italy – then plunged 150ft (46m) to his death. "He slipped on the wet grass," said his wife, "and went over the side." A police spokesman added: "It's just not lucky for everyone." *D.Mirror, 20 Nov 1992.*

STUBBORN ARMANDO PINELLI, 70, WON his argument with another man over who should sit in the only chair in the shade of a palm tree in Foggia, Italy – then died when the tree fell on him. *Sun, 18 June 1993.*

THE ANNUAL PILGRIMAGE TO THE AMARNATH cave, 12,725ft (3,878m) up in the mountains of Kashmir, claimed at least 214 lives in August 1996 because of heavy snow and rain, landslides and freezing temperatures. Some 112,000 Hindus came to Kashmir for the pilgrimage to the cave's icy stalagmite, which is regarded as a lingam (phallus) of the god Siva. *[R] 28 Aug 1996.*

CZESLAW B, 60, WHO WAS SO AFRAID OF burglars he filled his house with lethal booby traps, fell victim to his own safeguards. He was found shot dead outside his garage on 19 November 1996, killed, according to initial investigations, by two home-made guns mounted on the garage doors. Explosives experts, moving cautiously through his house in Kosianka Trojanowka village, eastern Poland, found eight similar traps by the front door, in rooms and in the attic. Each device was fitted with a discreet off-switch. There were 28 more booby traps in the house in various stages of construction. *[R] 20 Nov 1996.*

RALPH BREGOS, 40, WAITED TWO YEARS for a heart transplant. When news arrived at his Kentucky home that a donor was available, he got so excited that he had a massive heart attack and died. *D.Record, 9 Feb 1996.*

IN AN ATTEMPT TO CURE MARIA MENDOZA'S fear of heights, psychiatrist Ed Cabrillo took her up 20 floors of a Brazilian office block and told her she had nothing to worry about – just step into that lift. Maria bit her lip, took a pace forward, and plunged to her death. They hadn't noticed the warning signs that the lift was under repair. *The People, 31 Oct 1993.*

POLLY PERRY, 54, DECIDED TO MAKE A parachute jump to help overcome her fear of heights; but died on her first attempt. She was harnessed to an instructor during a tandem jump at Santa Fe, New Mexico, and they fell 8,500ft (2,600m) to their deaths when the main parachute failed to open. *Augusta (GA) Chronicle, 6 April 1994.*

TWO RUSSIAN POLICEMEN SHOT EACH other dead on 7 March 1997 in a case of mistaken identity while trying to arrest suspected robbers. One group of policemen in the town of Nizhny Novgorod east of Moscow mistook another group for the crooks in the dark after they refused an order to drop their weapons. *The Times (Malta), 11 Mar 1997.*

ON 27 AUGUST, A 40-YEAR-OLD LORRY DRIVER left his home in the town of Ordes in northwest Spain, planning to walk 20 miles (32km) to Caion so that he could give thanks at the shrine of the "Virgin of Miracles" for his recovery from a road accident a year earlier. A mile into his pilgrimage, he was knocked down by a car and killed instantly, as were his two aunts who were walking with him. An Ordes police spokesman said that the driver of the car had probably fallen asleep at the wheel, and that an investigation had been opened. *[AFP] 30 Aug 2011.*

CHARLES DAVIES, 67, FROM CHELTENHAM in Gloucestershire, sang the old soldiers' song 'Goodbye' at the annual dinner of the Cotswold Male Voice Choir in Eckington, Hereford and Worcester, on 23 January 1995. He finished with the words: "I wish you all a last goodbye". As the crowd applauded, he collapsed and died. *Sussex Eve. Argus, 23 Jan 1995.*

RICHARD VERSALLE, 63, DIED WHEN HE FELL 10ft (3m) from a ladder onto the stage of the Metropolitan Opera House in New York on 5 January 1996 during the opening scene of 'The Makropulos Case', Janacek's opera about the secret of eternal life. It was thought that he had suffered a heart attack. Versalle, who was alone on stage at the time, was portraying a law clerk named Vitek and was climbing a ladder to return papers to a filing cabinet. Somewhat ironically, the last line he sang, in the English translation of the original Czech, was "Too bad you can only live so long", a reference to a protracted lawsuit that was finally about to be settled. Versalle fell to the stage, landing on his back with his arms outstretched. The curtain was swiftly lowered and he was rushed to hospital, but was dead on arrival. *[AP] 5 Jan; NY Post, 6 Jan 1996.*

A 79-YEAR-OLD JAZZ MUSICIAN MAKING her theatre debut as a spirit passing into heaven played her last note and died on stage of an apparent heart attack on 15 November 1996. Deedie Ball performed in the play, then collapsed at the piano while playing a musical introduction for the next act. "It was the most beautiful death I have ever seen," said Karen Hammon, a friend in the audience. *[AP] 19 Nov 1996.*

HAVING GIVEN A SPEECH TO A toastmasters' club in Johannesburg in which he advised his audience to "enjoy life while you can, because death could strike at any moment", Danny du Toit, 49, collapsed and choked to death. *Guardian, 4 Mar 1997.*

A TOTAL OF 58 PEOPLE DIED AND AT LEAST 100 were injured in stampedes at two Hindu shrines involving worshippers who gathered to pray for protection on 15 July 1996, an unlucky day according to astrologers. About 35 of the fatalities occurred at the Siva temple complex in Ujjain in the central state of Madhya Pradesh. Some of the victims were crushed, while others were impaled on a bamboo barricade. *Eastern Eve. News, 15 July; Halifax Eve. Courier, 16 July 1996.*

MOUNTAINEER GERARD HOMMEL, A veteran of six Everest expeditions, fell off a ladder while changing a light bulb in Nantes, France, in October 1993. He cracked his head on the sink and died. *The People, 10 Oct 1993.*

AT LEAST 118 MUSLIM PILGRIMS DIED in a stampede on the last day of the *haj* at Mina, outside Mecca in Saudi Arabia. Around noon on 9 April 1998, pilgrims were performing a ritual known as "stoning the devil", which involves throwing seven chickpea-sized stones at each of the three pillars at Jamraat on the Mina plain three times over three days. Each pillar symbolised one of the temptations of Satan. Some elderly and ill pilgrims fell off the Jamraat bridge; most deaths occurred in the ensuing rush. An estimated 2.3 million pilgrims from about 100 countries took part in the 1998 *haj*.

On 2 July 1990, 1,426 pilgrims were crushed in a tunnel stampede in Mecca; on 23 May 1994, 270 died in a stampede during the "stoning the devil" ritual; and on 15 April 1997, 343 pilgrims died when a fire swept through 70,000 tents at Mina. *[AP] 9 April 1998.*

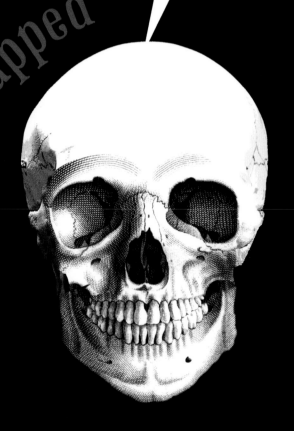

CHAPTER 2

Zapped

The powers of nature are awesome when unleashed.
And in the case of electricty, they have proved
deadly time and time again...

A POACHER DIED AFTER HE TRIED TO CATCH fish by putting a live cable into a pond outside Moscow. He forgot to disconnect the electricity before collecting the fish. *D.Record, 16 June 1994.*

FLORIAN IORGA, 42, AND HIS SON AUREL, 16, were electrocuted by a booby-trap they had set up to protect their onion patch in Bucharest, Romania. Hearing noises in the night, they ran out to investigate – and tripped over the cables wired to the mains. The bodies were found by the man's wife. The same fate befell a 49-year-old man in Slatina, Croatia, earlier in the year after he wired up his house and its perimeter against burglars. *(Scottish) Sunday Mail, 12 June; Europa Times, April 1994.*

TO SUPPORT HER AMPLE FRAME, BERBEL Zumner, 23, wore a bra reinforced with metal wires. These conducted a bolt of lightning that killed her as she was walking through a park in Vienna. *D.Record, 21 Oct 1994.*

TWO MUSLIMS IN WESTERN NIGERIA went to offer special prayers at Sobi Hill after the Eid-al-Adha feast at the weekend of 27/28 April 1996. A storm broke out and in a display of divine ingratitude, the two men were struck dead by lightning, while four others were knocked unconscious. *Daily Graphic (Ghana), 3 May 1996.*

 A BULLET FIRED INTO THE AIR IN celebration by villagers on their way to a cattle show in the northern Pakistani city of Rawalpindi on 29 June 1996 brought down a high voltage power line, killing at least 15 people and four water buffalo. *[AP] 1 July 1996.*

A FIREWORKS ROCKET SLAMMED INTO A high voltage cable on 14 August 1996. It fell on a crowd in Peru, killing 35 people and injuring at least 50 others as revellers celebrated the 456th anniversary of Arequipa, Peru's second largest city. The cable hit a crowd watching the festivities from a bridge. Some people burst into flames as 10,000 volts surged through them. The previous February, Arequipa was the scene of Peru's worst-ever air crash, which killed 123. *[AP] 16 Aug 1996.*

LAURENCE BAKER, A MURDERER JAILED IN 1983 who had been spared the electric chair in 1987, was electrocuted in a Pittsburgh jail when he sat on a stainless steel commode while watching television and wearing a set of badly wired homemade headphones. The accident happened between 10pm on 1 January 1997 and 1.30 the following morning.

It was an eerie re-run of the death of Michael Anderson Godwin, 28, on 6 March 1988. Godwin was a murderer who escaped the electric chair in Columbia, South Carolina. While sitting naked on the metal commode in his cell, he electrocuted himself by biting through a wire while mending the headphones on his TV. The headphones were required to prevent the sound from disturbing other prisoners. *[AP] Philadelphia Daily News, 3 Jan 1997; [UPI] 8 Mar 1988.*

 PATRICIA NOSIGLIA, 22, DIED ON 26 MAY 1998 when she picked up her phone in Buenos Aires, Argentina, and received a 13,000-volt shock that knocked her to the floor. Police said an electric cable had crossed the telephone line running from the street to the house. *[AP] 28 May 1998.*

STEPHEN ROONEY'S FATHER WAS KILLED by a bolt of lightning in 1963 while he was fishing in Fortescue, New Jersey, when Stephen was five years old. After seeing lightning in the sky during a barbecue in Hammonton, New Jersey, on 10 July 2011, Stephen said to his family and friends: "Don't worry guys, lightning never strikes twice." He then stepped away from the barbecue with his cousin Scott Digeralamo to smoke cigars by a tree, when lightning hit the ground where they were standing. Digeralamo survived the strike, but Rooney died five days later. *NBC Philadelphia, 13 July 2011.*

ERICA MARSHALL, 28, WAS MONITORING a horse receiving oxygen therapy when it became alarmed and kicked through the wall of the pressurised hyperbaric chamber, used to speed up injury recovery. Its steel horseshoe created a spark, causing a huge blast that threw debris 1,200ft (365m) and could be heard 30 miles (48km) away. Part of the roof and the side of the chamber was ripped off in the explosion, killing the horse and Mrs Marshall, who was watching it via a video link in a nearby room. Mrs Marshall, who married last November, had been running the chamber at the Kentucky Equine Sorts Medicine and Rehabilitation Center in Ocala, Florida, for two years and had treated between two and six horses a day. Her last patient had not been tranquillised as it had been inside the chamber four times previously and had not reacted adversely. *D.Telegraph, Times, 14 Feb 2012.*

CHAPTER 3

Animal Tragic

From an enraged ostrich to a camel with revenge on
its mind, members of the animal kingdom can turn
homicidal with alarming frequency...

DEREK ROMERO, 15, OF COMMERCE CITY, a suburb of Denver, was found crushed to death on a bedroom floor with a 11.5ft (3.5m) Burmese python, Sally, coiled next to him. The snake, which belonged to the victim's elder brother, was quite agitated and hissed at the police. It had been in the house for eight years, and had no history of attacking people. Since it had been fed a rabbit about five days earlier, it was unlikely that it was seeking prey. The family's theory was that Romero had forgotten to wash his hands after playing with a pet rabbit – a definite no-no, since snakes hunt by smell. *[R] Rocky Mountain News (CO), 21+23 July 1993.*

THREE FIJIAN FISHERMEN CHOKED TO DEATH on live fish, all within a few weeks. All had tried to kill their catch by biting its head. A fisherman from the island of Rabi was the first fatality in December 1994. On 14 January 1995, a fish head lodged in the throat of Samueal Taoba, 50, from a village on the island of Vanua Levu. Its spines lodged in his gullet and he suffocated before his friends could pull it out. Serupepeli Lumelume, 22, died in exactly the same way on 14 February, while fishing in a river near Narvosa on the island of Viti Levu. *[R] 16 Jan, 17 Feb 1995.*

MERIKE ENGELBRECHT, 25, FROM TZANEEN in South Africa, was kicked to death by a giraffe as she walked her dogs in a game park near Musina in the north of the country. She died instantly after one of her German shorthaired pointers startled the giraffe, which had a calf nearby. "It looks like she scooped up one of the dogs and tried to protect it," said family friend William Smith. "That's when the giraffe kicked her on the back of the neck." *Metro, 13 May 2010.*

A SHEEP TO BE SACRIFICED FOR THE MUSLIM feast of Al-Adha rushed its executioner, who lost his balance and fell to his death from the top of a four-storey building in Cairo in 1997. Another case of sheepish self-defence in Egypt was reported in 2001. Destined for sacrificial slaughter, it forestalled its owner's plans by pushing him to his death from a three-storey building in Alexandria. Waheeb Hamoudah, 56, who worked in the police tax evasion department, had been feeding the sheep he had tethered on his roof on New Year's Day when it butted him. He had been fattening it for six weeks in anticipation of Eid al-Adha, the Muslim feat of sacrifice, in early March. Neighbours found Hamoudah bleeding and unconscious on the ground, with several broken bones. He died soon after reaching hospital. *Sunday Telegraph, 20 April 1997; [R] 3 Jan 2001.*

FOURTEEN PATIENTS, INCLUDING FOUR newborn babies in incubators, died after a rat gnawed through the wiring of Catarino Rivas hospital in San Pedo Sula, northern Honduras, cutting off electricity. Six died when the power to their life-support machines was cut. The short circuit killed the rat. *[AP] 26 Aug 1997.*

OUMA (OR ANNA) HENDRIKS, 63, WAS attacked by an enraged ostrich on a farm in Joostenbergvlakte, about 25 miles (40km) outside Cape Town. Her husband Abraham, 65, watched helplessly as she was kicked and stomped on for about an hour. He managed to flag down help after the ostrich left, but Mrs Hendriks died in hospital four days later. The attack occurred on 22 December 1997 when the couple, who lived on an adjacent farm, walked through an ostrich herd at the Lekkerwater farm on their way to visit friends. *[AP] 29 Dec 1997.*

A CAMEL HERDER AT JIZAN in southern Saudi Arabia paid with his life for beating one of his beasts, the *Al-Iqtissadiya* newspaper reported. The camel waited all day after the morning beating before trampling the sleeping herder to death and biting his neck. The blood-stained camel was shot dead after the herd's owner found the body. *Adelaide Advertiser, 27 Sept 2000.*

A FIGHTING COCK APPEARED TO HAVE TAKEN deadly revenge on its owner for forcing it back into the ring too soon. It attacked Singrai Soren and slit his throat with the metal blades attached to its legs. One of the dead man's friends in the West Bengal village of Mohanpur, known only as Desai, said: "The cock tried to get away from the ring several times, but Soren pushed it back repeatedly. This upset it and it attacked him." Fighting cocks are usually given a break of at least an hour before facing another opponent, he explained. "Most masters are satisfied with the cash reward of £28 for every fight and a dead opponent to feast on." A few days later, on 30 January 2011, a cock stabbed Jose Luis Ochoa, 35, in the leg with a blade attached to its leg at an illegal cockfight in Tulare County, California. Ochoa died in hospital about two hours later. *D.Mail, 20 Jan; (London) Evening Standard, Independent, 8 Feb 2011.*

DANILO MAGGIONI, 38, SHOT A WILD boar near his home in Varese, northern Italy. Searchers later found both the hunter and hunted dead – the enraged boar had attacked Maggioni and hurled him into a ravine before dying. *Sunday Express, 10 Dec 1995.*

JUDSON NEWTON, 43, WENT BOATING with friends off Jaw Beach on New Providence Island in the Bahamas on

29 August 2010 and had engine problems. (The beach was so named because one of the *Jaws* movies was filmed there.) Rescuers found three men aboard who said that Mr Newton and another friend had swum to shore. Neither of them was found until fishermen caught a 12ft (3.6m) tiger shark on 4 September and cut it open. Human remains were found in its stomach and identified as belonging to Mr Newton by fingerprints. *Metro, 17 Sept 2010.*

A FARMER IN SOUTH AFRICA WAS KILLED by his pet hippopotamus on 12 November 2011 after repeated warnings that it could never be tamed. Marius Els, 41, an army major, was bitten to death by the 1,200kg (2,646lb) hippo he named Humphrey and tried to domesticate on his farm near Klerksdorp in Free State province. Els's body was found in the river where, years earlier, the hippo had been rescued from a flood. It was bought by Els at the age of five months and became a pet on his 400-acre (160ha) farm, learning to swim with humans. Els kept 20 different species of exotic animals, including giraffe and rhino. Earlier that year, he was photographed riding on the five-year-old hippo's back. "Humphrey's like a son to me, he's just like a human," he had said. *D.Telegraph, 14 Nov; Guardian, 15 Nov 2011.*

GOLFER DAVID BAILEY, 40, OF CLONDALKIN, Co. Dublin, was killed by a rat that ran up his trouser leg as he hunted for a lost ball at Caddockstown golf course in Co. Kildare. He startled the animal when he jumped into a ditch at the first hole. It shot up his leg and urinated on him. His playing partners advised him to take a shower immediately, but he laughed off the encounter, saying he had no cuts or bites. He took a shower four hours later after finishing the round. However, before this he had touched his leg and smoked a cigar. Doctors believe that the deadly Weil's disease carried by the rat was passed from his fingers to his mouth. Two weeks later, he was admitted to a Dublin hospital with severe jaundice, and he died in intensive care when his kidneys collapsed. *D.Mirror, 30 Aug 1996.*

FELIX DE LUIS MORETIN, 74, WAS GORED TO death when a bull charged through his front door after escaping during a festival in Lodosa, Spain. He died instantly when the bull's horn pierced his neck as he was sitting in his holiday home in the town of Navarra. *D.Telegraph, 4 Aug 2011.*

A PRIZE BULL THAT KILLED A FARMER MAY have been spooked by an unfamiliar hat he was wearing. Ian Rook, 58, wore his new red bobble hat instead of his usual flat cap in the bitter cold, and had not approached the field in his usual car. He suffered fatal chest injuries when the two-ton Aberdeen Angus threw him in the air and trampled him at his farm in Clanfield, Hampshire, in November 2010. Farm workers pulled the father of two away while the bull stood "snorting over the red hat". The bull, whose horns had been removed to reduce aggression, was destroyed. (The fact that Mr Rook's hat was red was probably of no consequence, since bulls can't see colour well.) *D.Mail, Metro, Sun, 16 Feb 2012.*

GIANT RATS AS BIG AS CATS killed and ate two babies in separate attacks in South Africa on 30 May 2011. Lunathi Dwadwa, three, was killed as she slept in her family's shack in the Khayelitsha slum outside Cape Town. She was sleeping on a makeshift bed on the floor of the breezeblock and corrugated iron home when she died. Her puzzled parents didn't even hear her scream. When

Bukiswa Dwadwa, 27, discovered her daughter's body, she saw that her eyes had been gouged out. "She was eaten from her eyebrows to her cheeks," she said. "Her other eye was hanging by a piece of flesh." Her father Mncedisi Mokoena said police told him: "Nothing could have done that but rats." The other baby was killed in Soweto township near Johannesburg while her teenage mother was out with friends. She was arrested on charges of culpable homicide and negligence.

The deaths appeared to be part of a spate of deadly rat attacks in the country. In April, 77-year-old grandmother Nomathemba Joyi died after giant rats chewed off the right side of her face. Township residents say the African Giant Pouched Rats – native to sub-Saharan Africa – grow up to 3ft (90cm) long, including their tails, and have front teeth over an inch long. They are nocturnal, omnivorous, and can produce up to 50 young a year. Some tribal people breed them for food. *dailymail.co.uk, 3 June; Sun, 4 June 2011.*

A PYGMY ELEPHANT FATALLY GORED AN Australian tourist at the remote Tabin wildlife reserve on Borneo island on 7 December 2011. It was the first known fatal attack in Malaysia's eastern Sabah state. The wild male elephant had been roaming alone around a mud volcano when Jenny O'Grady Donley, 25, a friend and their Malaysian guide saw it while trekking near their resort. Donley, a vet, is believed to have gone within 10m (33ft) of the animal, which may have charged at her because it was alarmed by the unfamiliar humans. Pygmy elephants are unique to Borneo. *[AP] 9 Dec 2011.*

ON FRIDAY THE THIRTEENTH, APRIL 2012, A PATIENT at Darent Valley Hospital in Dartford, Kent, was kicked and bitten to death by a stallion as she took a walk on doctor's orders. The unnamed 53-year-old from nearby Gravesend was repeatedly attacked by the horse, thought to belong to travellers, as she crossed a field. Walkers found her mauled body five hours later with the horse still standing over her. It had to be tranquillised so that police could recover the victim. Her death was not treated as suspicious and the horse was not put down. *D.Telegraph, Sun, 15 April 2012.*

A BOY OF 15 DIED AFTER CRASHING HIS BICYCLE into a deer that jumped out in front of him. Ben Madden suffered serious head injuries in the accident on a country lane near his home in Brough, East Yorkshire. He died on 31 July 2011 after four days in a coma. It was unclear whether he was wearing a helmet or not. *D.Telegraph, 3 Aug 2011.*

AN ANGRY SWAN WAS BLAMED for knocking a man out of his kayak in a Chicago pond and then continuing to attack until he drowned. Anthony Hensley, 37, worked for a company that used swans and dogs to keep geese away from properties. He was in a kayak checking on the birds on 15 April 2012 when one of them attacked. By the time rescuers arrived, Hensley had drowned. Investigators believed he had gone too close to the swan or its nesting area. *Chicago Sun Times, 16 April; ABC News, 17 April 2012.*

CHAPTER 4

What are the Odds?

A mother and son drop dead at the same moment.
Two men picking cherries fall from ladders and die
simultaneously. Coincidence? Or the
skeletal hand of fate?

 ON THE MORNING OF 8 NOVEMBER 1995, Vittorio Veroni was killed on the Via Cartoccio level crossing in Reggio Emilia, northern Italy, when his Renault 21 was hit by a train and carried along the line. His daughter Cristina, 19, had been killed four years earlier, on 19 January 1991, at the same crossing, by the same train, driven by the same driver. The crossing, over the Guastella-Reggio line – unmanned and without any protective bar, the legal norm for Italy's local railways – was near a bend in flat landscape and the morning sun can be dangerously blinding. It was bright on the mornings of both deaths.

Signor Veroni, 57, a builder from nearby Novellara, drove back and forth to work several times a day over the crossing. Suggestions that he decided to take his life at the place where his daughter died were repudiated by his family and the train driver, Domenico Serafino. Investigators said his death was accidental. They believed he was either blinded by the sun or was hindered from turning to look before crossing because of a plaster cast he wore around his chest following a workplace accident. *La Repubblica (Italy), 9 Nov; D.Telegraph, 10 Nov 1995.*

 HERMAN LORENZ, 88, WAS KNOCKED DOWN and killed by a train at a crossing in the Chicago suburb of Northbrook on 13 January 1996. Witnesses said he went round the crossing gates and kept going after the Amtrak train engineer sounded a warning horn. In October 1926, Lorenz had survived a crash at the same crossing. A train sliced though the school bus he was riding, killing two people, including his seatmate. *[AP] 16 Jan 1996.*

 TWO MEN WHOSE BODIES WASHED ASHORE in Monmouth County, New Jersey, on 3 April 1997 shared a birthday the following day. Robert Wolf of Highlands would have

been 24 and Jesse Bostik of Asbury Park, 81. Wolf's body was found in Eagles Nest Bay and Bostik's about eight miles (13km) south. Both drowned. *Newark (NJ) Star Ledger, 5 April 1997.*

HELMUT SIMON, 67, FAILED TO RETURN from a climb on the 2,467m (8,094ft) Gamskarkogel in the Austrian Alps on 15 October 2004. Eight days later, his body was found in a stream at an altitude of around 2,200m (7,218ft), apparently having fallen 100m (328ft). The sudden heavy snowfall that killed him was unusual weather for the time of year. The retired caretaker from Nuremberg had discovered Ötzi the Iceman during a mountain hike with his wife Erika on 19 September 1991. The location was the Similaun glacier in the Tyrolean Ötz Valley on the Austrian-Italian border. The tattooed body of the shaman-hunter, later determined to be 5,300 years old, was hailed as one of the most extraordinary Neolithic finds ever made.

After lengthy and costly court battles, the Simons had recently been awarded £50,000 for finding the Iceman, who was making a lot of money for the museum in Bolzano and the South Tyrol tourist industry. Mr Simon had returned to Austria for a walking tour to celebrate winning the award, but he had not signed the deal, so his widow never received a penny. It took the couple until 2003 to be legally recognised as the finders – a year to the day before Mr Simon disappeared. Dieter Warnecke, head of the rescue service that found Mr Simon, died of a heart attack an hour after Mr Simon's funeral.

The deaths encouraged mutterings concerning a "Curse of Ötzi". Dr Rainer Henn, 64, who placed the mummy in a body bag, was killed in an unexplained road accident in 1992, on his way to give a talk about the Iceman. Mountain guide Kurt Fritz, who led Dr Henn to the mummy, was the only one of a group of climbers killed in 1993 in an avalanche on a slope he knew well. Rainer Hölzl, who filmed the discovery for Austrian television, developed a brain tumour that killed him at the age of 47 a few months later. Prof Konrad Spindler, head of the Iceman team at Innsbruck University, died in April 2005, apparently from complications arising from multiple sclerosis.

The supposed curse claimed a seventh victim in October 2005. Dr Tom Loy, 63, director of the Archæological Sciences Laboratories at the University of Queensland's Institute for Molecular Bioscience, was found dead in his house in Brisbane, Australia, as he put the finishing touches to his book on the world's oldest mummy. His body lay undiscovered for several days. For about 12 years, he had been suffering from a hereditary condition that caused his blood to clot, a condition diagnosed shortly after he became involved with the mummy. The autopsy results were inconclusive, apart from ruling out any suspicious circumstances. "We have been told he died of natural causes or an accident, or a combination of both, but Tom was in poor health," said his brother Gareth.

It should be pointed out that since more than 150 scientists had come into contact with the mummy in the 14 years since its discovery, from a statistical standpoint seven deaths is not exceptional. The idea of a "mummy's curse" dates back to two stories: *The Mummy* (1821) by Jane Loudon Webb and *Lost in a Pyramid: or, the Mummy's Curse* (1869) by Louisa May Alcott. The supposed "curse of Tutankhamen" was promoted by the novelist Marie Corelli. *D.Telegraph, 19 Oct; [R] 23 Oct; [AFP] 25 Oct; Metro, 9 Nov 2004; The Australian, 4 Nov; Independent, 5 Nov 2005.*

STEPHANIE BREEDING, 17, DROWNED IN Seattle on 12 September 1998 when the car in which she was a passenger crashed through a guardrail on the Evergreen Point floating

bridge. The two young men she was with managed to swim to safety, but she was trapped inside. She was a cancer survivor who, at the age of nine, had received a heart transplant from someone called DJ who had drowned in a ditch with his friends. In May 1997, Breeding and her mother appeared on the *Oprah Winfrey Show* in which she and other organ recipients were introduced to relatives of their donors. *Sun (Bremerton, WA), 16 Sept 1998.*

ON 28 JUNE 2000 A 69-YEAR-OLD MAN in Vögisheim near Müllheim in Germany fell off a ladder while picking cherries. He died in a Freiburg hospital the following morning at the same time as a 68-year-old man in Ebringen, only six miles (10km) away, who fell off a ladder while picking cherries and died immediately. *Der Rebland-Kurier (Müllheim), 5 July 2000.*

ON 19 AUGUST 2001, A COUPLE'S three-year-old son drowned in a lake near Gonvick, Minnesota – the same lake where the couple's small daughter and son had drowned three years earlier. Arne and Carol Kleppe had adopted their son Alex from Russia after their other two children, Arla (four) and Anders (two) drowned in Six Lake in November 1998. The lake is near a farm owned by the children's grandmother. Alex disappeared while playing with the family dog as his parents were milking cows. *[AP] 24 Aug 2001.*

A MOTHER AND HER SON DIED APPARENTLY of natural causes within a short time of each other in their living room in Brighton, East Sussex. Charlotte Major, 82, and Clifford Parsons, 45, were found slumped in armchairs with the radio on. Police broke into their house in April 2003 after being alerted by a neighbour who had not seen them for a while. A television guide was open at 25 February. Police initially suspected murder, but tests showed that Mrs Major died of heart failure while her son, a heavy drinker, succumbed to alcohol poisoning. *D.Mirror, 12 April; Metro, 22 May 2003.*

 TWO FRIENDS DIED OF HEART ATTACKS at exactly the same time as they sat chatting over cups of coffee. Doctors were said to be baffled. Stanimir Dmitrovic, 64, and Slavko Banzic, 66, both suddenly complained of chest pains before collapsing in Banzic's house in Nevade, northern Serbia. Checks on the coffee established it wasn't poisoned, and medical professionals said there were no suspicious circumstances. *Sun, (Dublin) Metro, 19 June 2008.*

 MOBILE PHONE NUMBER 0888 888 888 was suspended after all three users assigned it in the previous 10 years died prematurely. First there was Vladimir Grashnov, former CEO of Bulgarian mobile phone company Mobitel which issued the number, who died of cancer in 2001 aged just 48. There were persistent rumours that his cancer had been caused by a business rival using radioactive poisoning. The number then passed to Bulgarian mafia boss Konstantin Dimitrov, who was gunned down aged 31 by a lone assassin in the Netherlands during a 2003 trip to inspect his £500 million drug-smuggling empire. The Russian mafia was thought to have been behind the killing. The number then passed to Konstantin Dishliev, an estate agent and major cocaine trafficker, who was gunned down in 2005 outside an Indian restaurant in Sofia, the Bulgarian capital. He died after a consignment of the drug valued at £130 million was intercepted by police on its way into the country from Colombia. Since then, the phone number has

been dormant while police maintained an open file on Dishliev's killing. Now phone bosses have suspended the number for good. Callers now get a recorded message saying the phone is "outside network coverage". *D.Telegraph, 26 May 2010.*

OTECHESTVEN FRONT IS A BULGARIAN television show featuring people who have done extraordinary things, but after six of its guests met with strange deaths, bosses at Nova TV were considering cancelling the programme amid whisperings that it was cursed. The first victim – a brutal former crook identified only by his criminal nickname Marin "The Rose" – simply collapsed and died within days of appearing on the show in 2009. Another victim was "miracle mum" Ivanka Arsova, 62, who had a statue of the Virgin Mary that cried real tears. Two days after the show, a stranger appeared at her door and said God was "calling her". A local newspaper reported: "Within a week she had died of undiagnosed cancer. She had seemed perfectly healthy until then."

Other victims include a disabled charity worker, a former prostitute and a drug addict who committed suicide on the way home from filming. The latest victim, herbalist Halil Baev, died in April 2011 when he rushed back into his burning house to save his black cat. "We are aware of what is being said about the show and we are looking into it," said a channel spokesman. "It might be that we need to change the format." *Metro, 4 May 2011.*

IAN GAMBLE, 16, WAS STABBED TO DEATH on 24 February 1996 after an argument with some youths as he walked through the grounds of Barnard Castle, Co. Durham. A few yards away was a memorial to his brother Darren, who was killed in an accident in March 1988, also at the age of 16. Darren and his friend Steven Laybourn were sitting in a car in the garage of Steven's home with the engine running to keep warm; but they fell asleep and were killed by the exhaust fumes. *D.Telegraph, 26 Feb 1996.*

POLICE IN CALGARY, ALBERTA, WERE CALLED on 2 August and found a 29-year-old man dead from multiple stab wounds. James Karl Bach, 54, was arrested and faced a charge of manslaughter. Bizarrely, the victim's name was Brent Stabbed Last. *cnews.canoe.ca, 3 Aug 2011.*

CHAPTER 5

Decapitations

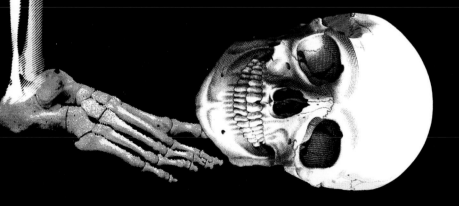

Keeping your head isn't easy - especially in a world of flying manhole covers, malfunctioning lifts and whirring helicopter blades.

NORTH SEA OIL WORKER ELLARD ZUIDEMA was decapitated by a helicopter's rotor blades on the diving support ship *Mayo* in April 1992. Mr Zuidema, 6ft 3in (1.9m) tall, ducked to avoid the blades, but a huge wave caused the *Mayo* to shudder and the blades dipped to 5ft 8in (1.7m). *D.Telegraph, 5 Nov 1992.*

INVENTOR HECTOR PENNA SPENT FOUR years developing a powerful factory cooling fan. His was modifying his invention in his laboratory in San Julian, Argentina, when his wife walked in and turned on the light switch, not realising he had connected it to the fan. He was decapitated by the blades. *D.Record, D.Star, 9 Jan 1995.*

WELFARE CLERK JAMES CHENAULT, 54, boarded a lift in the Kingsbridge Welfare Center in the Bronx, New York, with four others on 6 January 1995. The lift raced up to the second floor, apparently out of control. When the doors opened, Chenault straddled the doorway to allow the others off. One made it out, but with the doors still open the lift resumed its climb, decapitating Chenault. His head, wearing stereo headphones, fell into the lift with the three remaining passengers while his body fell down the shaft. *[AP] 7 Jan 1995.*

EDWARD MUSGROVE, 32, ATTACKED his estranged wife as she began an evening route as a Los Angeles bus driver. He grabbed the steering wheel, causing the bus to veer off the road, hit a tree and crash into a brick wall. The wife was not injured, but Musgrove was hurled through the windshield into the wall and decapitated. *Los Angeles Times, 17 Aug 1994.*

A HEATWAVE IN EGYPT CLAIMED ITS strangest victim when high temperatures caused a chemical explosion in a sewer, blowing off a manhole cover which decapitated 12-year-old Rami Farag Khalaf as he worked at a garage painting cars in the Delta town of Al-Santa. Paint run-off from the garage had reacted with the chemicals in the sewer under the intense heat, building up gas pressure that finally blew off the lethal lid. *Middle Eastern Times, 12-18 May 1996.*

ALEXANDRA GREER, 13 MONTHS, STRAPPED in a forward-facing child safety seat while being driven by her mother, Rebecca Blackman, in Boise, Idaho, was decapitated by a car airbag when the car collided with another vehicle at slow speed. The child's head was blown out of a side window. Airbags inflate at up to 200mph (320km/h) and had by that time been blamed for the deaths of at least 30 children. *[R] 29 Nov 1996.*

AN ASIAN TAXI DRIVER FROM MANCHESTER tied one end of a rope around his neck and the other to a nearby lamppost, then drove off one evening in December 1996 in his Toyota Carina. Security guards, investigating why the taxi was still there the following morning with its engine running, found the driver's head a short distance way, still attached to the rope. *Taxi Globe Trade, Dec 1996.*

CUI TINGXUN, A TEACHER IN CHINA'S Shandong province, was practising the esoteric healing art of qigong with his wife when he suddenly attempted to gouge out her eyes, saying he had received instructions from a 'greater being' to change her facial features. Cui then attacked his wife's jaw with his teeth, saying her mouth smelled bad, before decapitating her with a meat cleaver. Police found him holding the shoulders of his wife's torso, exhorting her to sprout a new head. *Hong Kong Eastern Express, 7 May 1996.*

WHITESON MWANDIYA, 55, WAS BEHEADED when a giant pane of glass sliced through his neck as he unloaded it. He was in a six-man team removing the delivery from a truck in Kitwe, Zambia, when it began to topple. His colleague Richard Kasongo, 40, also died after suffering cuts all over his body. The other four were unhurt. *D.Mirror, 10 Nov 2011.*

CHAPTER 6

Toxic Terminations

Poisonous caterpillars, noxious seaweed,
odd allergies and midget wrestlers
killed by eye-drops

FIVE CHILDREN DIED AND ANOTHER 150 people were taken ill after eating the flesh of a 40kg (88lb) mystery sea creature that looked like a turtle. It was caught by a Vietnamese villager in the northern province of Quang Binh. *South China Morning Post, 16 Jan 1994.*

KATHY TAGUE DIGIROLAMO, 29, FROM Hatfield, Pennsylvania, suffered from bronchial asthma and an allergy to shellfish. On 13 November 1994, she had trouble breathing after a waiter walked by her table in a restaurant with a steaming platter of shrimp. Her asthma inhaler was ineffective, her breathing worsened and, despite medical attention, her pulse rate plunged and her heart stopped. Such deaths merely from smelling certain foods are the result of a system-wide breakdown called anaphylactic shock and are exceedingly rare. *Omaha (NB) World Herald, 4 Dec 1994.*

AN EGYPTIAN WOMAN ACCIDENTALLY PUT rat poison instead of pepper on her 18-year-old daughter's lunch, killing the young woman on the day before her wedding. Um Hashem Abu Mahmoud died after suffering severe stomach pains. The family lived in Koum Hamada, 80 miles (130km) northwest of Cairo. *ITV Teletext, 30 Nov 1996.*

A BRAZILIAN WOMAN OF 52 DIED IN October 1996 after brushing her arm against a caterpillar. Death by caterpillar is now three to six times more common than by snakebite in southern parts of the country (at least 10 fatalities in the previous three years). The killer caterpillars, *Lonomia obliqua*, have hairs containing poison with anticoagulant properties. The woman felt burning of the skin, headache and weakness. Over the subsequent two days, she developed bruising and vomited. She was hospitalised in a coma and tests showed she suffered bleeding in the brain. She died two days later. The caterpillar population had been growing in rural areas because rats, birds, wasps and their other natural predators had been killed by rapid deforestation and the use of toxic fertilisers. *Independent, 11 Oct 1996; Guardian, 6 Jan; Observer, 14 Jan1997.*

IN MAY 2010, JURORS WERE CONSIDERING the case of a New York City man who received a donor kidney and died in what experts said may be the only known case of uterine cancer transmitted by transplant. The widow of Vincent Liew sued NYU Langone Medical Center over his 2002 death. Mr Liew was told six weeks after the transplant that the female donor had uterine cancer, but decided to keep the kidney after his doctor said the risk of getting the disease was small. He had the kidney removed about six months later, but within weeks he died of cancer that his autopsy showed had come from the donor. *(Sydney) D.Telegraph, 29 May 2010.*

CHRISTOPHER "PASQUAL" NORRIS, 50, died from septicæmia in Edinburgh Royal Infirmary on 8 July 2006; post mortem tests showed that anthrax was the most likely cause. Mr Norris, a Buddhist who lived alone in an isolated house in Stobs, near Hawick in the Scottish Borders, made sculptures, bongos and decorative items, importing untreated animal skins – from which he presumably breathed in the deadly anthrax spores. His home was sealed off and recent visitors were told to seek medical advice in case they had touched infected hides. However, anthrax doesn't pass from person to person so there was no reason to suppose the public was at risk.

This was the first human case of anthrax in Scotland since 1987, although there was a scare at a farm in Lennoxtown, East Dunbartonshire, where a cow was thought to have died from the disease in 2002. Anthrax spores can survive dormant for years, especially in soil. An infection can be treated with antibiotics if identified early enough. Gruinard Island off the western Scottish coast was out of bounds for decades after it was used for secret anthrax germ warfare experiments in 1942, only being declared safe in 1990. The last known human death from anthrax in the UK was in 1974. *Edinburgh Eve. News, 16 Aug; Times, 17 Aug 2006.*

 A PREVIOUSLY HEALTHY 47-YEAR-OLD welder from Buckinghamshire was admitted to hospital with fever. Within 24 hours he became so short of breath that he was placed in intensive care. Tests showed he was suffering from "overwhelming sepsis", a condition which led to kidney problems, low blood pressure and a fast heart rate. After being referred to a specialist regional centre and put on a heart-lung machine, the man's condition worsened, leading to kidney failure and death. Blood samples showed aspergillosis, a reaction to the common fungus, *Aspergillus fumigatus*. The man's partner revealed he had developed symptoms within 24 hours of being engulfed in "clouds of dust" while he "dispersed rotting tree and plant mulch in the garden". Dr David Waghorn, who treated the patient, wrote in *The Lancet*: "Acute aspergillosis after contact with decayed plant matter is rare, but may be considered a hazard." The fungus grows on dead leaves, compost heaps, and in stored grain. Experts warned people handling organic waste to wear facemasks. *Independent, (London) Eve. Standard, 13 June 2008.*

TWO PROFESSIONAL MIDGET WRESTLERS found dead in a low-rent Mexico City hotel room on 29 June 2009 were fatally drugged by a female robbers posing as prostitutes to attract victims. The 36-year-old twin brothers were Alberto and Alejandro Pérez Jiménez. They began their fighting careers 17 years earlier in a tag team called The Small Devils and sometimes crossed over into American WWF/WWE wrestling. Alberto went by the name La Parkita (Little Death), and wore a skeleton costume in the ring. Alejandro was known as El Espectrito II (Little Ghost), and also fought at WWE events using the alias 'Tarantula'. They picked up the two women after filming a TV fight show and had their alcoholic drinks spiked before being robbed.

Tests suggested they hadn't had sex with the women. It is thought their small stature (4ft 1in/124cm) made them more vulnerable to the drugs, although larger men have died in similar crimes. At their funeral, tearful mini-wrestlers donned their professional costumes to form a guard of honour. Mexican police said 20 people were arrested for similar crimes in 2008. By tracing calls made on one of the midgets' mobile phones, they arrested a 65-year-old woman, accusing her and an accomplice ("The Fat One") of spiking the wrestlers' drinks with eyedrops. Surveillance cameras showed the two women leaving the hotel. [AP] 2 July; Metro, 3+22 July; Sun, 4 July; BBC News, 22 July 2009.

 A 48-YEAR-OLD LORRY DRIVER WHO DIED on a beach in northern France in July 2009 might be the first victim of toxic seaweed fumes. He had carried three truckloads of sea lettuce away from the beaches at Binic in Brittany where it had been decaying, releasing poisonous hydrogen sulphide gas. He was part of an annual operation to clear 2,000 tons of sea lettuce from the beaches. He had been working without a mask or gloves and died at the wheel of his vehicle when it crashed into a wall. Although the cause of death was originally given as a heart attack, French scientists subsequently believed that he might have been killed by the toxic fumes. The alarm over the algæ was raised after a horse galloping along the beach at Saint-Michel-en-Grève collapsed and died. Its rider lost consciousness and had to be dragged from a metre-deep patch of rotting green sludge. *D.Mirror, 8 Aug; [R] 8 Sept 2009.*

IN APRIL 2009, DIEUDONNE MASHA AND a neighbour were walking home along the shores of Lake Kivu in eastern Congo after an evening of drinking when they encountered two soldiers who asked to see their ID cards. Mr Masha didn't have his on him, so he ran away and hid in a rocky ditch. His body was found there the following morning; there were no signs of violence. As if the citizens of Goma and environs don't have enough to worry about – what with cannibalistic mercenaries, famine, ebola, volcanic eruptions, and the world's greatest frequency of lightning – Lake Kivu harbours vast reservoirs of potentially lethal methane and carbon dioxide.

Mr Masha is believed to have died instantly when he hid in a bubble of carbon dioxide, known in Swahili as a *mazuku* ("evil wind"). Nearly 100 people every year die from the carbon dioxide vents along the lake's northern shore. Stories of people feeling breathless and light-headed while swimming in the lake are common, and could account for many of the drownings there. In the aftermath of the Rwandan genocide in 1994, many died from *mazukus* that sent clouds of gas into jam-packed refugee camps along the lake.

The eruption of Mount Nyiragongo near the lake's northern shore in 2002 stimulated interest in the gas fields beneath Lake Kivu's surface: 300 billion cubic metres (392 billion cubic yards) of carbon dioxide and 60 billion cubic metres of methane slowly building towards saturation point, or potential release. Similar events have been recorded at least twice, both times on lakes in Cameroon in the 1980s. In one case, more than 1,700 people were killed. However, the volume of gas under Lake Kivu is much larger. *Int. Herald Tribune, 7 Nov 2009.*

A FIVE-YEAR STUDY BLAMED AN innocuous-looking mushroom known as Little White for many mysterious deaths in south-western China. No one knew what caused Yunnan Sudden Death Syndrome, blamed for an estimated 400 deaths in the past three decades. However, an investigative team from China's Centre for Disease Control and Prevention (CDC) announced that Little White is responsible for the baffling condition, which strikes remote villages in the rural highlands of Yunnan province every summer.

More than 90 per cent of the deaths occurred in the rainy season (June to August), and at an altitude of 5,900-7,900ft (1,800-2,400m). "We heard amazing stories about how people would drop dead in the middle of a conversation," said Zhang Shu, a cardiologist who took part in the CDC study. "About two-thirds of victims, in the hours before death, experienced symptoms such as heart palpitation, nausea, dizziness, seizures and fatigue."

The investigation was initially hampered by language barriers and the remote location of the villages. However, in 2008, the scientists noted that the Little White mushroom was often found in the homes of the people who died. Yunnan province is well known for its wild mushrooms, many of which are exported at high prices. Families, who make their living by collecting and selling fungi, eat the Little White as it has no commercial value – it is too small and turns brown shortly after being picked. The mushroom belongs to the Trogia genus and has three toxic amino acids (which are not used in proteins); the scientists conjectured that these became lethal when consumed with barium, a heavy metal found in high concentrations in the local water supply. By 2010, a campaign to warn people against eating the tiny mushrooms had dramatically reduced the number of deaths. *[AP] BBC News,14 July 2010.*

 A WOMAN DIED AFTER AN ALLERGIC ATTACK thought to have been triggered by a dentist's mouthwash. Sacha Rumaner,

30, from Brighton, was having her teeth cleaned on 2 February and was not even under anæsthetic when she went into anaphylactic shock. Dental staff said she had complained of feeling hot and having an itchy leg moments before she lost consciousness. She was pronounced dead before she could be taken to the Royal Sussex County Hospital nearby. A consultant allergist said serious reactions to mouthwash were very rare, but could be caused by a chemical antiseptic, chlorhexidine, which is used in some brands. *D.Mail, Metro, 23 Mar 2011.*

Dumb Deaths

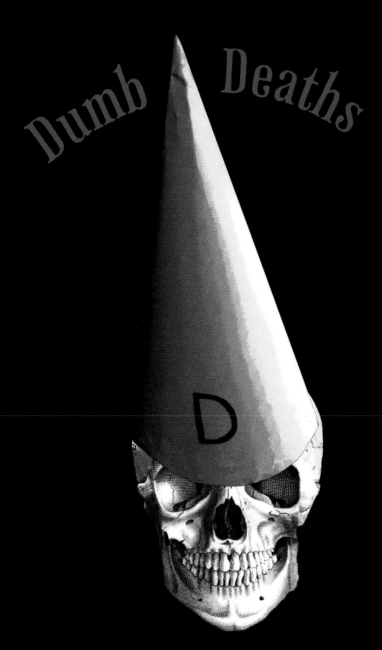

Some people seem determined to help evolution by removing themselves from the gene pool – the idiotic exits in this chapter are perfect examples...

FARMER ISMAIL AYYILDIZ TOLD drinking companions in the western Turkish province of Edirne that he would shoot out an aching tooth on 8 September 1995 – but the DIY dentistry proved fatal when the bullet left his mouth via the top of his head. He was rushed to hospital, but died a few hours later. *[R] 9 Sept 1995.*

A TURK IN COPENHAGEN CELEBRATING A Christmas Eve wedding by firing a gun into the air killed two guests and wounded nine. The man, whose 12 shots bounced off a concrete ceiling, forgot he was indoors. He was charged with manslaughter. *[R] 27 Dec 1995.*

CHIANG HOCK GOAN, 22, A SINGAPOREAN disc jockey also known as DJ Suave, was killed on 6 January 1996 in Kandal province, north of the Cambodian capital Phnom Penh. According to *Cambodia Daily*, he had asked a soldier to shoot at him to test the protective powers of a talisman he wore. *(Sydney) Herald-Sun, 10 Jan 1996.*

EGYPTIAN FARM WORKER SUSU BORAI Mohammad, 22, accidentally swallowed some ants when she took a swig of water. She went home and drank some insecticide to kill the ants, but suffered diarrhoea and convulsions and died immediately after being taken to hospital in the Qena district of Cairo. *D.Record, 30 Sept; Middle East Times, —Dec 1996.*

IN AN APPARENT CASE OF OSTENSION (contemporary legend becoming actual news), wealthy Charles Felder, 71, died after his cleaner, 47-year-old Pauline Jassey, unplugged his life-support machine

to use the vacuum cleaner in his bedroom in Dallas, Texas. *D.Record,
7 Mar 1998*.

D ANTHONY ERVIN MUST HAVE THOUGHT that robbing a blind man would be easy; but Courtney Beswick, aged 28 and blind since birth, flipped him over his shoulder and put him in a wrestling hold until police arrived. Ervin was taken to hospital in Philadelphia, but was pronounced dead of neck injuries. In 1987, Mr Beswick was named Most Valuable Wrestler for the Eastern Atlantic Association of Schools for the Blind. *Guardian, 12 Oct 1996*.

D IVAN TODOROV, A 35-YEAR-OLD RUSSIAN computer programmer who had been dumped by his girlfriend, died after persuading a friend to bury him alive overnight, hoping it would bring him "good luck". He dug a hole in a garden in the far eastern city of Blagoveshchensk and climbed into an improvised coffin, with holes for air pipes, taking with him a mobile phone, a blanket and a bottle of water. His friend covered the coffin with planks and 8in (20cm) of earth and then left, after Todorov phoned to say he was fine. However, sludge from heavy overnight rain clogged the air tubes and the next morning his friend returned to find him dead.

Numerous Russian bloggers had written of undergoing supervised self-burial. State newspaper *Rossiiskaya Gazeta* had even run a feature on the practice. In the summer of 2010, a man in the Vologda region of north-western Russia persuaded a friend to bury him in a forest to help him overcome his fear of death. He was found dead an hour and a half later, crushed by the weight of earth. *BBC News, D.Telegraph, 2 June; Sun, 3 June 2011*.

D THE BODY OF HENRY CARLTON, 41, WAS found on 5 February 1996 wedged halfway through a window of a real estate agency in Williamsport, Pennsylvania. His legs were inside and his head and arms outside, and a bag of burglary tools was next to him. He apparently believed he could squeeze through the 15in (38cm)-high, 18in (45cm)-wide window and drop to the floor; but the window was obstructed by a heating duct and Carlton's bulky clothes stopped him. He froze to death. *[AP] 7 Feb 1996.*

D ELDERLY GOLFER JEAN POTEVAN THREW HIS golf bag into a lake after missing three putts on the final hole of a disastrous round in Orleans (or Lyons – the reports disagree) in France. Realising that his car keys were in the bag, he waded in fully clothed and drowned when he got entangled in weeds as he dived under the water. According to fellow player Henri Levereau, his last words were: "I'm going back for the keys, but I'm leaving the clubs down there." *Sunday Express, 14 May; D.Mirror, 19 May 1995.*

D WELDER SVEN LUND DIED TRYING TO THAW his car's fuel line with a blowtorch. Police in Stockholm said: "He was a very good welder, but didn't know a lot about cars." *D.Star, 29 April 1994.*

CHAPTER 8

Unexplained Exits

Some deaths defy explanation, leave
the police baffled and would need the talents of a
Sherlock Holmes to unravel their mysteries...

? THE BROOKLYN UNION GAS COMPANY tried for months to gain entrance to a house in 110th Street, Forest Hills, Queens, to read the meter. On 1 December 1994, workers arrived with a locksmith and a city marshal. They entered the basement, where they found a corpse behind a huge cobweb, seated on a patio chair near the boiler. The deceased was identified as Long Lu Lee, 69, a retired mechanical engineer. His head had dropped off and was found beneath the chair. His widow, Thuc Khoanh Lu, 62, told police that her husband had disappeared the previous winter, but that she had never filed a missing persons report. She seemed genuinely surprised to learn that he had been dead in her basement all year. She was not considered a suspect in his death. *NY Daily News, 2+4 Dec; BT (Denmark), 4 Dec 1994.*

? TWO BEACHCOMBERS FOUND A BLOCK OF ice encasing the naked body of a man at Roedvig, south-eastern Denmark. Police didn't think the man – aged 20 to 25 and with Asian features – had been murdered as there were no signs of wounds. They also considered suicide unlikely, as suicides don't usually strip. The body had been in the ice for several weeks. *[AFP] 28 Feb 1996.*

? ALL FIVE MEMBERS OF BRAZIL'S HOTTEST rock band died in March 1996 when their plane crashed into a hill above Guarulhos, their hometown, near São Paulo airport. The Mamonas Assassinas (Killer Mammaries) were returning from the final concert of a five-month tour. The previous December, the São Paulo soothsayer Mother Dinah predicted in the Daily *Folha da Tarde* that they would be involved in a plane crash. Hours before the last concert, hair salon owner Nélson de Lima videotaped keyboard player Júlio Rasec as he was having his hair dyed red. "Last night I dreamed something," said a concerned Júlio on the tape. "It seemed the airplane was falling."

As they boarded the plane that night in Brasilia for the flight to Guarulhos, a runway worker wished them luck in their forthcoming overseas debut: "I hope you're a smash in Portugal." Replied lead singer Dinho Alves: "It's my head I'm going to smash." *Time, 18 Mar 1996.*

? ANGELA WAGSTAFF, 34, A FORMER NURSE at Bristol's Southmead Hospital who had drink and mental health problems, was found dead at her home in Hereford after an injection of between 1,000 and 3,000 units of insulin. Such a massive overdose would have needed about 20 syringes to administer, but she only had one puncture mark on her right hip and no syringe was ever found. There were no signs of a struggle. David Walwyn, who shared his home with Mrs Wagstaff, denied killing her. In July 1996, the Hereford coroner recorded an open verdict. "There seem to be so many inconsistencies," he said. *Western Daily Press, 3 July 1996.*

? CRIME WRITER AND FORMER STEEL WORKER Eugene Izzi, 43, was found hanged from his office window in Michigan Avenue, Chicago, on 7 December 1996. There were three computer disks in his pocket that contained his latest work. Like Izzi, the central character in this 800-page novel is a Chicago mystery writer with a 14th-floor office. In both fact and fiction, the victim was hanging from a rope anchored to a metal desk in the office. The writer and his character were both wearing a bullet-proof vest, both carried a set of brass knuckles and a can of mace, and both had a loaded .38-calibre on the floor of the office. In the book, however, the hero hoists himself up the rope and shoots his assailants, members of a secret Indiana militia.

Friends said that Izzi, who sometimes wrote under the name Nick Gaitano, had received death threats from a militia group that he had infiltrated. "He let me listen to the voice mail," said Bob Rice, a former

Chicago homicide detective. "A woman said he'd been found guilty…
and he'd be dead by hanging by the end of the year." Police found
transcripts of other threats in Izzi's office. However, they ruled out foul
play – Izzi's office door was locked from the inside – and speculated that
the author, a stickler for accuracy, was trying out his own plot device.
Alternatively, as he was undergoing treatment for depression, he might
have committed suicide, leaving a mystery as a legacy. In the end, the
Cook County coroner decided it was suicide, although many of Izzi's
friends couldn't accept this. "I just don't see him doing that," said Hugh
Holton, a Chicago police lieutenant. "He had a book coming out, a wife
and children – he had a lot to live for." *Boston (MA) Globe, 14 Dec 1996,
9 Jan 1997; Hackensack (NJ) Record, (Cork) Examiner, 9 Jan; USA Today,
17 Jan 1997.*

❓ A SIX-YEAR-OLD BOY COLLAPSED IN THE playground at
Coley Park Primary School in Reading, Berkshire, on 14 January
1998. Despite attempts to resuscitate the child, he died at the Royal
Berkshire Hospital. "There were no visible injuries," said a police source.
A year earlier, on 20 January 1997, eight-year-old Joanna Canlin collapsed
and died in the same playground. No cause of death was ever established. *(London) Eve. Standard, 15 Jan 1998.*

❓ THE REMAINS OF A MAN WHO HAD BEEN missing for
27 years have been discovered lodged in the chimney of a bank
in Louisiana. Joseph W Schexnider, who was 22, disappeared from the
town of Abbeville in January 1984, after missing a court hearing over
charges of possessing a stolen vehicle. His mother said at the time that
he had been known to leave abruptly – including once to work with a
circus – and was this time thought to be on a "rendezvous". However,
human remains were discovered with a pair of gloves, a cigarette lighter,

a watch and a wallet in a chimney during renovations at Abbeville National Bank in May 2011. DNA tests in July confirmed that the remains in the chimney, which was sealed off later in the 1980s, were those of Schexnider. He probably died of dehydration or starvation. He had no bag with him, so the police do not suspect him of trying to rob the bank; so what on earth was he doing in the chimney? *D.Telegraph, 27 July 2011.*

ON 15 MARCH 2011, A TREE SURGEON working on behalf of London's Royal Parks visited West Island, a tree-covered piece of land at the end of St James's Park nearest to Buckingham Palace, usually inhabited only by wildfowl. After clearing away some leaves, he uncovered a clothed skeleton next to some vodka bottles and a decayed yellow cushion. One of the bottles was tied to the clothes with string. The bones turned out to belong to Robert James Moore, a 69-year-old American; a pathologist estimated that they had been there for about three years. Moore had sent hundreds of "strange and offensive" packages to the Queen over a period of 15 years, including obscene photographs. Some of the "peculiar" letters ran to 600 pages, and he had also posted a copy of his passport and boxes falsely warning that they contained dangerous substances.

It is thought that the royal family was unaware of his obsession, as all their mail is screened. In 2007 Moore arrived in Britain from the US, where he had been in trouble with the police for drink-driving. The only way to reach West Island is by wading or swimming across the shallow lake. Moore could have camped out there for weeks or even months. Several forms of ID were found in his pockets, including a US passport that matched the copy once sent to the Queen. At the inquest in Westminster in late September, Dr Fiona Wilcox, the coroner, commented on the "excellent, unimpeded view of the palace" from the island and recorded a verdict of "unascertained" cause of death. No next-of-kin have been located and he was not on any missing persons list.

The details of Moore's life drew comparisons with the famous case of a Frenchwoman who thought George V was sending her signals by moving the curtains in Buckingham Palace. As *Daily Telegraph* columnist Christopher Howse pointed out, St James's Park historically is just the place for a hermit. When it was being re-designed in the early 18th century, William Kent constructed for Queen Caroline a hermitage called Merlin's Cave. This rum cross between a grass-roofed African hut and a gothic ruin was installed in the gardens of Richmond Lodge. The Queen then appointed Stephen Duck, "The Thresher Poet", as her ornamental hermit. "Ornamental hermits were quite the thing in the Age of Reason," commented Howse. "No grotto was complete without one." *(London) Eve. Standard, 3 Oct; D.Telegraph, 3+4 Oct; dailymail.co.uk, 4 Oct 2011.*

CHAPTER 9

Deadly Drives

Our roads are dangerous places at the best of times - and that's before you factor in falling ice, flying bears or escaped emus...

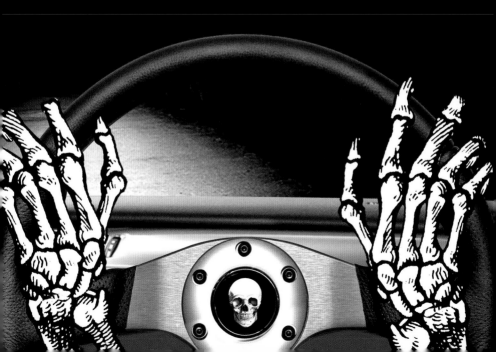

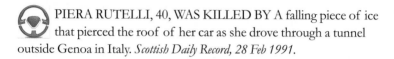 PIERA RUTELLI, 40, WAS KILLED BY A falling piece of ice that pierced the roof of her car as she drove through a tunnel outside Genoa in Italy. *Scottish Daily Record, 28 Feb 1991.*

MRS EVELYN HOUSER, 70, DRIVING near Waynesburg, Pennsylvania, struck an embankment and overturned. She escaped unhurt. As she stood near a guardrail while police investigated, she was fatally injured by a 16-year-old firefighter who lost control of his car on the way to the accident. *Belfast Telegraph, 19 Mar 1992.*

DAVID WAYNE GODIN, 22, DROWNED near Dartmouth, Nova Scotia, in September 1992 as he was returning from his bachelor stag party, when his vehicle plunged into a lake. Attached to Godin's leg, courtesy of his friends at the party, was an authentic ball and chain. *Hartford (CT) Advocate, 3 Dec 1992.*

CHARLES MILLBANK, 25, CRASHED INTO an electricity pole on the A127 near Brentwood on 22 January 1993 and plunged over an embankment. He escaped unhurt, scrambled up the embankment, touched the 11,000-volt cable trailing across the grass and was killed instantly. *Independent, Today, 23 Jan 1993.*

IN JULY 1993, STEPHEN CAWTHORNE, 43, a former district engineer from York, died from head injuries when his Yamaha 600cc motorbike was jumped on by an emu in a narrow cutting near Mount Surprise, Queensland. A week earlier, on 16 July, motorcylist Kelly Cordry, 39, was killed when a 40lb (18kg) black dog fell on him from a railway bridge in Commerce City, Colorado. The motorbike slammed into the crash barrier and Cordry was thrown into the path of oncoming traffic. *Denver (CO) Post, 17 July; [R] Sunday Express, 25 July 1993.*

THE SHARP THREAD OF A FLYING KITE slashed the throat and killed water engineer RC Senal in Orissa, eastern India, who was riding his motorbike to a meeting in Bhubaneshwar. War games with kites are a popular sport in India, and enthusiasts often put a paste of boiled rice mixed with glass dust on the string to cut the thread of other kites. Some kite flyers have sliced off their fingers in accidents. *[UNI] Hong Kong Standard, 18 Jan 1994.*

A GUM-CHEWING MOTORIST WAS KILLED after he blew a giant bubble that burst and stuck to his glasses, blinding him. Abner Kriller, of Albany, Australia, ran his car off the road and plunged down a hill. *Sun, D.Star, 25 June 1994.*

RACHEL DRAKE, 50, A HEAD TEACHER from Southampton, died instantly from massive head injuries when a 500lb (225kg) stag ran onto the road in front of her, was struck by an oncoming vehicle and landed on the roof of her car. *Huddersfield Daily Examiner, 10 Jan 1996.*

ANGIE JERSTON OF DENVER, COLORADO, was touching up her lipstick as she drove to work when she was forced to brake sharply. The tube shot into her mouth and stuck in her windpipe.

She died because she had locked the doors for safety and rescuers were unable to get in. *Weekly News, 23 Mar 1996.*

HELMUT MEZER, 18, FROM AUSTRIA, DIED in a high-speed car crash one week after getting his new driving licence and a BMW with the number-plate DEAD 1. The car skidded on a bend at 100mph (160km/h), hit a bank and catapulted through the air more than 200ft (60m) before landing on its roof in a field. Mezer was killed instantly and a friend in the passenger seat was seriously injured. *(London) Eve. Standard, 24 Mar 1997.*

TWIN 70-YEAR-OLD BROTHERS were killed on the morning of 5 March 2002 while riding bicycles on the same stretch of icy road near Raahe on the west coast of Finland. One twin was killed at a junction on Interstate 8 at 9.35am, 370 miles (595km) north of Helsinki, when he was run down by a lorry. At 11.47am, before police had identified the body and informed family members, the other twin was hit and killed less than a mile to the south by another lorry. The brothers were born in September 1931. One lived in Raahe and the other in Pattijoki nearby. They were not named. *[AP] Helsingen Sanomat, 6 Mar 2002.*

TWO SISTERS DIED WHEN THEIR MATCHING Cherokee Jeeps collided head-on at 60mph (97km/h) near Six Mile, Alabama, as they travelled to visit each other on 17 November 2002. Sheila Wentworth, 45, and her sister, Doris Jean Hall, 51, were killed, along with Mrs Hall's husband, Billy Joe, 45. Two children – one riding in each vehicle – were injured. The sisters would often visit each other unannounced and had travelled the country road countless times, mostly at weekends. *[AP] 20 Nov; D.Mirror, 21 Nov; Eve. Standard, 26 Nov 2002.*

 TWO BROTHERS WERE KILLED IN A HEAD-ON collision with each other in Michigan on 18 February 2007. Kessie (24) and James West (33) were killed when James lost control of his car and crossed into the path of his brother's car. *[AP] 21 Feb 2007.*

 TWO CANADIANS DIED INSTANTLY ON 6 JUNE when a Pontiac Sunfire hit a 440lb (200kg) black bear and sent it flying straight through the windshield of an oncoming vehicle and out through the back window. The bizarre accident took place around 10pm on Highway 148 near Luskville, Quebec. The deceased were a 25-year-old Ottawa woman driving a Nissan Pathfinder SUV and her friend, 40-year-old Steven Leon from Gatineau, Quebec, who was sitting on the back seat. Only the woman's 28-year-old boyfriend, in the front passenger seat, survived. The two men in the Pontiac Sunfire that initially hit the bear were unharmed. The adolescent bear was killed. The incident led to the intriguing Reuters headline, FLYING BEAR KILLS TWO CANADIANS IN FREAK ACCIDENT.

While rare, the region has seen at least one similar wildlife accident. In September 1994, Tracy Gourlay, 29, from Kingston, Ontario, was killed near Prescott, Ontario, when a 150lb (70kg) deer that was struck by another vehicle smashed through the windshield of a car being driven by her husband. The deer, just like the black bear, continued through the rear window. *Ottawa Citizen, 7 June 2011.*

 PHILIP A CONTOS, 55, RIDING BARE-HEADED on one of about 550 motorcycles in an anti-helmet law rally, lost control, went over the handlebars, hit his head on the pavement and died. The accident happened on 2 July in Onondaga, a town in central New York State, near Syracuse. Police said Mr Contos would probably have

survived if he had been wearing a helmet. He was driving a 1983 Harley-Davidson on a helmet protest ride organised by American Bikers Aimed Towards Education, or ABATE. The organisation states that it encourages the voluntary use of helmets but opposes mandatory helmet laws. Mr Contos, of Parish, hit his brakes and his motorbike fishtailed. He was pronounced dead at a hospital. *[AP] 4 July 2011.*

ROSEMARY BOWER, 70, OF BROOKVILLE, Pennsylvania, was driving on Route 830 in Washington Township at about 6.45am on 27 December 2011 when a car coming towards her struck a deer that ran into the road. The deer went airborne and hit Bower's windshield. The impact cut the animal in half and sent the head and shoulders into the car, killing Bower. Her car hit another car about 700 yards down the road before stopping in a ditch. The drivers of the other two cars were uninjured. No charges were filed. *[AP] 28 Dec 2011.*

By Their Own Hand

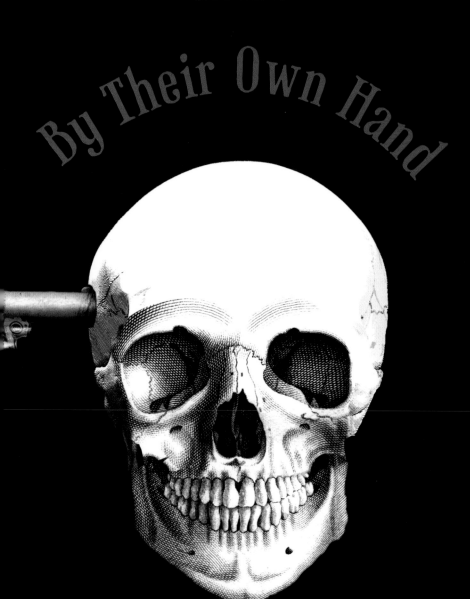

Taking their own lives seems to bring out people's inventive sides: here we have examples of suicide by jaguar, piranha and even a case of self-crucifixion...

CHAPTER 10   BY THEIR OWN HANDS

AN UNIDENTIFIED MAN IN HIS MID-20s told onlookers in Yamoussoukro, Ivory Coast, that he could no longer bear to live without President Felix Houphouet-Boigny, who ruled for 33 years until his death on 7 December 1993. The man jumped into the ruler's palace moat, drawing huge crowds who spent two days watching his body being devoured by crocodiles. *Hackensack (NJ) Record, 16 Feb 1994.*

A GUATEMALAN GUN SALESMAN COMMITTED suicide by hurling himself into a pit of jaguars in Guatemala City's zoo after accidentally shooting a customer dead. Paco Cazanga (32) was rescued from the pit by firefighters, who used fire extinguishers to repel four jaguars, but he died later in hospital. *Aberdeen Press & Journal, 1 Sept 1995.*

ANDREA RUGA, 47, HAD THE SAME NAME birthplace and date of birth as a Mafia godfather accused of terrorism and various kidnaps. Italy's police computer couldn't tell them apart and the "impeccably honest" ironmonger from Monasterace in southern Italy constantly had his house raided. At roadblocks, his wife and children sat weeping as he was hustled off to have his papers checked. At hotels, he suffered countless indignities as staff called the police. On 24 October 1995, he was found dead in a lay-by near Naples after taking poison. Minutes before, he had phoned three senators, three magistrates, a newspaper editor and the local police chief to say that he couldn't stand the aggravation any more. *D.Mail, 25 Oct 1995.*

AN 85-YEAR-OLD WOMAN COMMITTED suicide in Hunan province, China, when she started menstruating, because she thought, at her advanced age, it indicated demonic possession. *South*

China Morning Post, 8 Dec 1996.

 TWIN BROTHERS FROM CROATIA COMMITTED suicide on the same day without each other knowing. Branko Uhiltil, 57, hanged himself in his house in Lipovljani, 50 miles (80km) east of Zagreb; two hours later, his brother Ivan shot himself dead in his flat.
Aberdeen Eve. Express, 24 Mar 1997.

FAYE AND STEPHEN BEUBY, AN AMERICAN couple, bought a villa in the hilltop village of Benabbio, near the spa resort of Bagni di Lucca in northern Tuscany in 2000. On 30 November 2002, workmen broke through a bricked-up door to create space for a wine cellar, and found the skeleton of Nemo Cianelli, 57. With the skeleton lay a suitcase, rifle, bricklayer's trowel, bucket, pile of bricks and suicide note in a Chianti bottle.

The note, on paper headed with Cianelli's name, explained that he had decided to take his own life because he had an incurable disease and wanted to spare his family grief. In April 1958, he told everyone he was going to America and was never heard from again. He had evidently walled himself up in the basement and shot himself. He left detailed instructions with a local builder to come in after his "departure" and replaster the wall. The builder did so, never suspecting what lay behind the brickwork.

Cianelli had been a wealthy businessman who lived in the villa with his wife and daughters. He worked for a local tannery, drove a sports car and travelled frequently to America on business. His wife died several years earlier without learning what had become of her husband. His daughters had left the area. One has to wonder why none of them was curious about the new brickwork in the cellar.

An extra twist to the story was given by the family doctor, Francesco

De Paulis, who said that the medical records of Cianelli, whose first name means "no one" in Latin, showed that he had been in perfect health at the time of his disappearance. Even though the note was in Cianelli's handwriting, police are considering an alternative theory: that he was murdered and bricked in by his killer. *Times, Guardian, 5 Dec 2002.*

GRACE CAULFIELD, 37, WAS DISCOVERED dead in bed on Christmas Day 2006 after her concerned parents were unable to gain access to her flat in Dublin and alerted gardaí. A post mortem provided no anatomical cause of death and no drugs or alcohol were detected in her system. However, after strange seeds and a brown, tea-like substance were found in her flat, further tests were carried out and her blood and urine tested positive for taxine b, a highly toxic substance found in yew seed that can cause cardio-respiratory failure. An inquest concluded that Ms Caulfield had died after drinking a tea made from yew needles – an extremely rare way to die. The coroner felt unable to say for certain that she had intended to take her life and recorded an open verdict. *Irish Independent, 12 April 2008.*

DAVID WACKETT, 25, WHO WORKED AT the B&Q store in Bridgend, South Wales, tied a rope around his neck, fastened the other end to a tree and drove off at speed in his car. His decapitated body was found at 2am by a work colleague in the store's car park. *Sun, 9 Dec 2002.*

A LONDON TAXI DRIVER DECAPITATED HIMSELF on 10 July after tying a rope around his neck and a lamppost, and driving off at high speed in Great Suffolk Street in Southwark, just yards from a 24-hour café. The unnamed man, believed to be in his thirties, is said to have driven off in his black cab shortly after midnight, aiming straight at a pillar. His head was found some distance from his cab. *D.Mail, 10 July 2009.*

THERE WAS A VERY GOOD REASON WHY a man's body was not found in his car for a week: the vehicle had been buried under several feet of snow. Kevin Ronan, 36, from Long Island, was uncovered in the early hours of 1 February 2011 in Flushing, New York, after his brother recognised his car. He had apparently shot himself in the head with a shotgun, which was found on the seat beside him. The last time his family saw him was on 25 January when he stormed out of his relatives' home threatening to kill himself. He was reported missing that same day. *dailymail.co.uk, 1 Feb; NY Post, 2 Feb 2011.*

THE BODY OF A 58-YEAR-OLD TAXI DRIVER, surnamed Kim, was found in an abandoned stone quarry near Mungyeong, 115 miles (185km) southeast of Seoul in South Korea, on 1 May, a week after Easter. His hands and feet were nailed to a wooden cross, on his head was a crown of thorns, there was a wound on the right side of his torso, and he was wearing nothing but his underpants. Nylon strings were tied around his neck, arms and stomach, and there were whip marks on his skin. After carrying out a re-enactment, police believe he killed himself without assistance by nailing his feet to the cross, tying his neck to it and stabbing himself in the side. He is then thought to have drilled holes in his hands and slipped them over nails on the cross, which were hammered into the wood from the rear, leaving the sharp ends exposed. There were two smaller crosses erected on each side of the cross he was nailed to, as well as a propped-up mirror so the man could witness his own suffering. Not far away was a tent containing an electric drill, hammer, nails, pieces of wood and instructions for self-crucifixion in the man's handwriting. An SUV belonging to the man was parked nearby. An autopsy showed he had died of bleeding from the stab wound and suffocation. Acquaintances described him as a religious fanatic obsessed with out-of-body experiences, so perhaps he was hoping for resurrection. *Joongang Daily (Seoul), Times, 5 May; Dublin Metro, 6 May; D.Mail, 19 May 2011.*

A FARM WORKER IN SOUTH AFRICA IS thought to have committed suicide by wading into a river full of crocodiles after a quarrel with his girlfriend – although his sister refused to believe he had taken his own life and said he must have been pushed into the water. David Lubisi, a 40-year-old father of three, had not been seen for more than a week after apparently telling a colleague on 7 April 2011 about his plan to wade into the Lepelle River, near the town of Bushbuckbridge – close to the Kruger National Park in the eastern Mpumalanga province. A human leg was seen in a crocodile's mouth four days after his disappearance. *dailymail.co.uk, 18 April; Metro, Sun, 19 April 2011.*

FISHERMAN OSCAR BARBOSA, 18, BLED TO death in December after jumping out of his canoe into the Yata River in Bolivia, which was teeming with flesh-eating piranha. He suffered dozens of bites to his throat and face. Local police chief Daniel Cayaya believes that the teenager, from Rosario dei Yata in the northeast of the country, committed "suicide by piranha". Barbosa, who was thought to be drunk, knew the river well and would have been aware that it was full of red piranha at that time of year. The 14in (36cm) fish hunt in packs to strip their prey of flesh. They are known to devour large snakes and even jaguars in minutes. Fatal attacks on humans are rare, but swimmers at a river beach in Brazil were attacked by hundreds of piranha in September 2011. *Sun, 8 Dec 2011.*

Unusual Illnesses

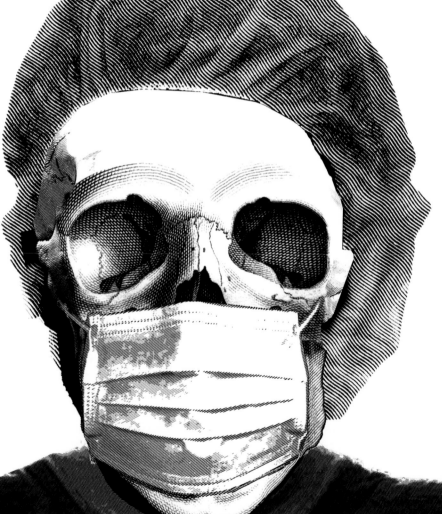

Our files are full of medical mysteries, baffling maladies and obscure but deadly disorders

MATTHEW MESSING, 16, WAS PLAYING ice hockey in Quincy, Massachusetts, one evening in 1995 when an opponent intercepted him with a routine bump to the chest. He collapsed on the ice and died instantly. The incident, along with nearly 70 others reported in recent years, had baffled doctors. In each case, they found no injury to the heart and no previous heart condition in the victims. However, the explanation for the rare deaths, which go by the medical name of *commotio cordis* – concussion of the heart – might have been found. Dr Gregory Kurfman and others suggested that the deaths resulted from an unusual conjunction of events. When the heart is beating, there is a fleeting moment, about a hundredth of a second long, when the electrical rhythm is resetting, so to speak, just before a beat. During that moment, if a moderate blow is directed to exactly the spot on the chest above the heart, the electrical rhythm breaks and the heart stops beating, fibrillating ineffectively. If the blow is too strong or too weak, or the timing is a few milliseconds off, death is averted. *New England Journal of Medicine, vol.338, no.25, 18 June 1998.*

A PÆDIATRIC NURSE DIED FROM HEART failure brought on by the shock of a ringing alarm clock, an inquest in Warrington was told on 28 April 2006. Lisa Jane Browne, 27, of Stoke on Trent, collapsed in bed on 10 January 1998, and was found by her husband at 7am. She had set the alarm clock for 6am but it was not ringing when he woke up. An inquest held at the time was inconclusive; but the Cheshire coroner, Nicholas Rheinberg, accepted that she had been suffering from a rare hereditary disorder called Long QT syndrome (LQT2). The condition affects the electrical system of the heart, which can cause sudden unexplained death in young people. The verdict of death by natural causes brought to a close an eight-year campaign by Lisa's mother to discover the true cause of her death. Lisa's father, sister

and two nephews were also found to have LQT2. They had all received treatment and were leading normal lives. *D.Mail, D.Telegraph, Western Mail, 29 April 2006.*

RICHARD LIGHTWOOD, 27, FROM RUGELEY, Staffordshire, collapsed and died while bowling for King's Bromley cricket club on 9 September 2006. His twin, Andrew, had died in 1994 while battling for a junior cricket side at the age of 14. Both had died at about 1.20pm from the same heart condition – hypertrophic cardiomyopathy – one that is rarely fatal. The condition is genetic, but a hospital consultant couldn't find a history of the diseases in the family when he examined the family tree. *D.Mail, 13 Sept 2006.*

FOUR TRANSPLANT RECIPIENTS – in Alabama, Texas and Oklahoma – died of rabies after receiving the organs of an Arkansas man. The link between the deaths only became clear in July 2004 after the source of the virus, extremely rare in the US, was tracked to a previously healthy 20-year-old Arkansas man who was admitted to hospital complaining of fever and confusion. He showed no symptoms of rabies and was thought to be suffering from a stroke. It later emerged that he had rabies, possibly from a bat bite. The disease sometimes doesn't develop for up to a year following a bite from a rabid animal.

On 4 May, following the man's death from a brain hæmorrhage, his kidneys and liver were transplanted into patients in Dallas. His lungs were sent to Alabama and used in a transplant, but the patient died soon after from complications following surgery. The four survivors developed symptoms of rabies within four weeks of surgery, becoming confused and lethargic and suffering muscle spasms. The liver recipient died on 7 June; the kidney recipients on 8 June and 21 June. The fourth victim, an unspecified organ recipient who also died some time in June, was only connected to the Arkansas donor after the 3 July report. It was the first known case of rabies being spread through donated organs, although at least eight patients had contracted it through cornea transplants. Rabies testing was not routine for US organ donors, although hospitals screened for HIV, hepatitis B and C, and syphilis. *Guardian, D.Mail, 3 July; Int. Herald Tribune, 10 July 2004.*

ERICA CRANMER, 74, WAS WALKING HER dog on Woodbury Common, near Exmouth in Devon, on 21 March 2006 when she scratched her arm on a gorse bush. From this she contracted the deadly flesh-eating bug necrotising fasciitis and died in the Royal Devon and Exeter Hospital on 29 March. Royal Marine cadet Richard Campbell-Smith, 18, was also a victim of Woodbury Common gorse. After a scratch there in November 2004, he died from Panton-Valentine Leukocidin, a toxin that attacks white blood cells and is linked to MRSA.

The Marines' training ground occupies part of Woodbury Common and many Marines developed a mysterious rash after training there. In March 2004, the Health Protection Agency reported 25 known cases of the skin irritation known as "Woodbury Rash". The explanatory legend round the barracks was that chemical and biological testing took place there during, or shortly after, World War II. Presumably, research could confirm this, or rule it out. *Western Morning News, 18 May; Western Daily Press, 19 May 2006.*

WHILE WALKING BAREFOOT IN NORTH-EASTERN Peru, a healthy Canadian woman, 22, stepped on caterpillars. She immediately experienced burning pain in her feet, which then radiated up her thighs. The pain worsened when she walked and she developed a headache. However, all symptoms resolved over the next 12 hours and

she didn't seek medical attention. Back in Canada, she did seek help after extensive bruises appeared on her legs. According to a report in the *Canadian Medical Journal*, doctors identified caterpillar envenomation and asked Brazilian authorities for advice. A local antivenene was immediately dispatched from Brazil, but by the time it arrived and was administered, the woman was already bleeding internally and it was too late to save her. *Australian Financial Review, 14 Aug 2008.*

ON HOLIDAY IN NORTHERN SCOTLAND on 23 May 2009, Steven Sewell was playing with his partially blind dog, Judy, while his son was fly-fishing. The retired teacher picked up a stick and was about to throw it when the 10-year-old Alsatian-doberman cross leapt up and bit his finger to the bone. He didn't wash the wound or put a plaster on straight away. On 29 May, he complained of feeling cold and shivery and the family made the 300-mile (480km) journey home to Hipperholme, Yorkshire, the following day. By the time they got back, Mr Sewell had started suffering from diarrhoea and loss of sensation in his fingers. He was taken to hospital, but died on 31 May from encephalitis, an acute inflammation of the brain. *Metro, 6 Nov 2009.*

RETIRED DESIGN ENGINEER JOHN ORAM, 79, sneezed so violently it caused his brain to bleed, resulting in his death in October 2009. Care home staff in Shaldon, Devon, had spotted him sneeze. Coroner's officer Ric Parsons said it was the first "death by sneezing" case he had seen. *D.Star, 24 Oct 2009.*

A NEW MOTHER WHO DIED SECONDS AFTER giving birth was suffering from a condition so rare none of her doctors had encountered it before. Julie Walsh, 28, died having suffered an amniotic fluid embolism, in which fluid surrounding her son in the womb entered her blood stream and caused an allergic reaction. *D.Telegraph, 4 Nov 2010.*

ROBERT FORD, 47, WAS SHOPPING WITH A friend in Gravesend, Kent, in June 2011 when his nose started to bleed. He walked into a medical centre for help. The bleeding soon stopped, and doctors advised him to go home and put ice on his nose. His father Michael told an inquest in December that when he phoned him later that day, Robert asked him to dial 999 because blood was beginning to clog his throat and he couldn't breathe. He was soon found dead at his home. His father said: "We found him on the floor with a small pool of blood around his mouth. There was also 10p-sized spots of blood around the house." Pathologist Olaf Biedrzycki said it was the only fatal nosebleed he had seen in 4,000 post-mortem examinations. "This was certainly as odd case," he said. "We don't really know how to explain it. I've looked very hard for a source of the blood and could not find it." The coroner recorded a verdict of death by natural causes. *D.Mail, 3 Dec 2011.*

SHY MARRIED COUPLE SACHI AND TOMIO Hidaka, both 34, waited 14 years to make love – and died of heart attacks the first time they tried it. They had no history of heart trouble, according to their doctor in Chiba, Japan. *D.Mirror, 11 Oct 1992.*

CHAPTER 12

Breathless

From the robber who choked to death on a stolen £50 bill to the stripper who suffocated inside a giant cake, lack of oxygen can be a killer...

OFF-DUTY BUS CONDUCTOR ABDUL Fadli Talib, 24, died after swallowing his dentures while sleeping on the back seat of a bus at it travelled from Kuala Lumpur to Seremban in western Malaysia on 21 September 1992. *[R] 23 Sept 1992.*

CABBIE ALLA DALHANNA'S HABIT OF chewing his sunglasses had fatal consequences. His car was rammed by another in El-Alamain, Egypt, and he choked to death. *(Scottish) Sunday Mail, 28 Mar 1993.*

IN AN ATTEMPT TO RESCUE A CHICKEN ON 31 July 1995, farmer's son Allam Sabet al-Sayyed, 18, descended a 60ft (18m) well in the Egyptian village on Nazlat Imara, 240 miles (390km) south of Cairo. He drowned, apparently after an undercurrent in the water pulled him down. When he failed to appear, his brother Sayyed, 20, climbed down to investigate… and drowned. Then his brother Ahmad, 16, climbed down and vanished – to be followed by their 14-year-old sister, Zeinab. Two elderly cousins arrived to see if they could help, but suffered the same fate. The bodies of all six were later pulled out, along with the chicken, which was the only survivor. *[AP] 1 Aug; Today, 2 Aug; Le Matin (Benin), 4 Aug 1995.*

HANS PENDER, FROM SALZBURG, AUSTRIA, suffocated when he became entangled in 60ft (18m) of thick wallpaper and couldn't struggle free. "The more he struggled, the tighter the paper wrapped him up," said detective Peter Dieker. *Sunday Express, 23 April 1995.*

A ROBBERY SUSPECT WHO TRIED TO swallow some incriminating evidence choked to death on a $50 bill. The man collapsed in the back seat of a patrol car in Buffalo, New York, on 25 April 1995 about an hour after he was caught attacking a woman in a supermarket parking lot. Nine days earlier in Australia, Adam Kane Morris, a 23-year-old paranoid schizophrenic from Kew near Sydney, had choked to death on a wad of 10 $50 bills which he swallowed during a fit in the bath. *Albuquerque Journal, 29 April 1995; (Sydney) Herald-Sun, 2 Mar 1996.*

MICHAEL P OLSON, 13, WAS FOUND DEAD by his uncle in the woods near his home in Eau Claire, Wisconsin. His entire head, including his mouth and nose, were wrapped in a large quantity of duct tape, and a roll of duct tape was found next to him. It as thought he had accidentally suffocated while experimenting with the tape. His family said he was obsessed with tape and had frequently wrapped GI Joe and Barbie dolls with it. *[AP] 12 June 1996.*

MOHAMMAD AL-ASSAD WAS FOUND DEAD in his bed (we are not told where). "There were no marks whatsoever on his body," said the coroner, "but the autopsy revealed large amounts of methane gas in his system. Relatives have confirmed to me that his diet consisted principally of beans and cabbage, exactly the right combination of foods to produce large quantities of methane. A neighbour heard what he described as 'the continuous sound of material being torn, followed by stifled screaming'." It appeared that the man had repeatedly passed wind and fatally gassed himself in his small air-tight bedroom. (This sounds unlikely if not impossible; but this is what the wire report states.) Rescue workers broke down the door and all three got sick; one had to be hospitalised. *[AP] 31 Aug 1995.*

PAUL FERGUSON, 25, FROM ECCLES, WAS found dead, stuck head-first down a fox hole in waste ground by Davyhulme sewage works, Stretford, near Manchester. He was out hunting rabbits with his six terriers and a ferret, and police believe he was trying to free one of the terriers, which was later found alive. He either suffocated or froze to death. Two months later, Philip Edwards, 26, from Edmondstown, Mid-Glamorgan, also died trapped head-first down a hole while trying to rescue his pet terrier. *Bradford Telegraph and Argus, 27 Jan; Eccles Journal, 30 Jan; Bristol Eve. News, 7 April 1992.*

STAG PARTY FRIENDS WERE CURIOUS WHEN a stripper failed to jump out of a huge cake in Cosenza, Italy. Then they found her dead inside it. Gina Lalapola, 23, had suffocated after waiting for an hour inside the sealed cake. *D.Record, 30 Aug 1997.*

BRIAN DEPLEDGE, 38, ASPHYXIATED WHEN he became trapped in the rungs of a clothes-horse at his home in Bradford on 1 February 2011. The father-of-two seems to have tripped over a stool and fallen backwards onto the dryer, trapping his neck and chest between its rungs as it collapsed. His efforts to free himself created a "cat's cradle" effect, which only made the compression worse. The clothes at the top of the dryer were still wet, which increased the pressure on his neck. Recording a verdict of accidental death, coroner Paul Marks said the incident was "probably rarer than being struck by lightning or a meteorite". *D.Mirror, Times, 10 Sept 2011.*

Murder and Mayhem

Since Cain slew Abel, murder has always been with us. Here are some particularly unusual offings, and a few unfortunate accidental killings too...

 ARTHUR PRATT, 65, OF MODESTO, California, died in hospital on 13 October 2002 six days after his wife Kelli, 45, held him down and bit him 20 times when he refused to have sex with her. "Most of the bites were confined to his arm and his abdomen and a few were very deep with major tissue damage," said Sgt Al Carter of the Modesto police. "He was able to dial 911 that night. We have a tape recording of him screaming while she was biting him. When officers arrived, he was screaming that he'd been assaulted. She fought with the officers and tried to bite them too."

Mr Pratt had been released from hospital several days before the incident. He suffered from diabetes, heart and circulation problems. Homicide charges against his wife were pending the outcome of toxicology results. *Los Angeles Times, Edinburgh Eve. News, 18 Oct 2002.*

TWO DOCTORS WERE CHARGED WITH murdering their son in October 2007 after transfusing his blood into an elder brother to make him more intelligent – advice given by a guru to the mother in a dream. The couple, from Rohtak, India, initially claimed the bright 10-year-old died in an attack. The 18-year-old, who had been struggling with his medical studies, was fighting for life in hospital. *Sun, 13 Oct 2007.*

CRAIG BUFORD, 19, OF FORT WORTH, TEXAS, was shot in the back on 3 October 1973 in a dispute with another teenager over gambling winnings, and spent several months in hospital recovering. Once healed, he had few lasting effects from his injures. He drove city buses in Denver and Seattle and later worked as a trucker before retiring. However, in December 2008, at the age of 54, Buford suffered a ruptured colon and died from multiple organ failure in Fort Worth hospital on the 29th. The Tarrant County medical examiner's office ruled the death a homicide, stating it was caused by complications from the gunshot wound 35 years earlier. Prosecution is unlikely because of double jeopardy issues; the youth had originally served a light sentence in a plea agreement.

Homicide rulings in such an old case are rare but not unheard of. In November 2001, the death of David Gunby of Fort Worth was ruled a homicide caused by complications from a gunshot wound he had received in August 1966, when Charles Whitman opened fire from the clock tower at the University of Texas at Austin, killing 16 and wounding 31. *Fort Worth (TX) Star-Telegram. 6 Jan 2009.*

A LAOTIAN MAN AGED 38 LURED HIS 24-year-old pregnant wife into a forest in northeast Xieng Khuang province on 3 January 2011 and killed her with an axe blow to the back. He told police he wanted to use the three-month-old fœtus to make a lucky charm called a "louk lord". He confessed to the police, telling them that he had heard that if he "produced a louk lord, he would be able to ask the ghosts for lucky lottery numbers". He refused to say what he had done with the fœtus. *MX News (Sydney), NY Post, 19 Jan 2011.*

JOSEPH NASO, 77, A PETTY THIEF and freelance photographer living in Reno, Nevada, was charged in April with the murder of four women in northern California between 1977 and 1994. He is said to have killed Carmen Colon, Roxene Roggasch, Pamela Parsons and Tracy Tafoya – who had nothing in common apart from their alliterative names. Detectives are trying to find out if Naso had anything to do with New York's "Double Initial Murders" – the killings in the early 1970s of three girls, each with matching initials. Spookily, one of them was also called Carmen Colon. However, authorities admitted that a DNA sample taken from one of the New York victims didn't

match Naso's and they have no physical evidence that he was involved in those killings. *Buffalo (NY) News, 14 April; Sun, 15 April 2011.*

AMATEUR FILM-MAKER MARK TWITCHELL, 31, went on trial in Edmonton, Canada, in March, accused of copying the gory plot of his own horror movie. The prosecution alleged that Twitchell posed as a woman on an Internet dating site in 2008, lured Johnny Altinger, 38, to a garage for a date, killed him, cut him up, dumped his body parts in a sewer and chronicled the crime on his computer. The plot of his movie, which he had completed a week earlier, involved a victim being lured to a garage and then being tortured to death. *MX News (Sydney), 18 Mar; Sun, 22 Mar 2011.*

RITA QUAM WAS COLLECTING ROCKS FOR her garden in Grand Junction, Colorado, when a man walked up in dark glasses, a black wig and a false moustache. He fired several shots from a semi-automatic pistol with a silencer, but they all missed. Then his gun jammed, so he tried to beat Quam over the head with large rocks. A policeman arrived and ordered the attacker to lie down; at this point he collapsed, his disguise fell off and he had a fatal heart attack. Quam then recognised him as Arthur R Smith, a retired Chicago police officer and an old friend of her ex-husband, Howard. *[AP] 15 Sept 1994.*

HU PAO-YIN, 35, STABBED TO DEATH HER mother-in-law on Christmas Eve. Her reason for this, she told police in Taiwan, was that "I am the most beautiful woman in the world and the existence of other women is unnecessary". Her adoptive mother survived a similar attack. *Western Mail, 16 Feb 1995.*

DUTCH STUDENT JIM TERWIEL, 26, WAS jailed for 12 years in 1995 after a psychotherapist said he had confessed to using a crossbow to fire a ballpoint pen through his mother's eye; but an appeal court in The Hague dismissed the testimony and said the woman had died in a freak accident, falling with the pen in her hand. *Western Morning News, 6 April 1996.*

A HUSBAND WHO DECAPITATED HIS WIFE because she refused to have children told a court in March 2010 that he was going through a "mid-life crisis". Postal Inspector Philippe Cousin, 53, killed his wife Nicole, 47, at their home in Arras, northern France, in April 2007. In 21 years of marriage, they had never had sex. She was a virgin and was afraid to have children in case they inherited multiple sclerosis from her side of the family. Cousin was sentenced to 18 years in jail. *Metro, 9 Mar; Sun, 11 Mar 2010.*

TWO WEDDING GUESTS DIED IN A GUN BATTLE in Aswan, Egypt, after the bride offended family honour by holding her husband's hand, breaking an ancient custom of not showing affection in public. *D.Mail, 27 Nov 1995.*

TWO MEXICAN PEASANT FARMERS, COUSINS aged 70 and 85, argued for years over water rights and finally faced off in an old-fashioned pistol duel in the western state of Jalisco on 8 March 2004. The bodies of Manuel Orozco and Candelario Orozco were found 11ft (3.4m) apart with one bullet wound each and the two handguns nearby. The cousins, who were also brothers-in-law, had long debated ownership of a water spring that Candelario used to irrigate a

small corn plot near the town of Pihuamo. The disagreement began to get out of hand when a water pipe broke recently. *[R] 11 Mar 2004.*

TWO UNDERTAKERS SHOT EACH OTHER dead in Paraiba, north-eastern Brazil, during an argument over who had the right to conduct the funeral of one of the town's inhabitants. Another undertaker from a neighbouring town was called in to bury all three bodies. *D.Telegraph, 28 July 1992.*

KARL WELKER, HUSBAND OF THE YEAR, battered his wife to death with his winner's trophy in Bonn, Germany. The businessman flew into a rage at the prospect of embarrassment when she said she was leaving him. Welker, 36, was jailed for 30 years. *D.Record, 8 Mar 1994.*

A BRICKLAYER WAS KILLED BY LABOURERS who cut off his head and burnt it in a kiln to redden their bricks, according to police in northern Bangladesh. Four suspects arrested over the 26-year-old's death claimed they acted on orders of the brickyard's owners, after a fortune teller recommended human sacrifice to turn the bricks red. *D.Telegraph, 22 Mar 2010.*

BEATRIZ ROBLEDO, 47, BECAME SO annoyed with her husband's hiccups as he was settling down for a nap that she tried to scare him – but the plan went horribly wrong. Nestor Lutz, 48, was so shocked when he opened his eyes and saw a figure crouching over him wearing a spooky carnival mask that he grabbed a knife and stabbed his wife to death. He then panicked and threw the body into a septic tank before turning himself in to police. The tragedy happened in the Argentinian town of Ituzaingo on 12 January 1997. *[AP] 16 Jan 1997.*

A STARTLED FATHER SHOT DEAD HIS 14-year-old daughter when she surprised him. Matilda Crabtree's parents, of West Monroe, Louisiana, had come home late when she jumped out of a cupboard shouting "Boo!" *(London) Eve. Standard, 9 Nov 1994.*

CARLOS JIMINEZ WAS FREED BY A COURT in Coro, Venezuela, after killing his wife Maria when he rolled over in bed and hit her with his elbow. *(Scottish) Sunday Mail, 28 April 1996.*

SIEK PHAN, 62, A VIETNAMESE WOMAN FROM the Cambodian province of Kompong Speu, was cutting firewood when her husband, Nou Meas, 65, sneaked up and tickled her. She instinctively threw her axe, killing him instantly. When she turned round she found she had nearly decapitated him. "I hate being tickled," she told the authorities. *[AP] 17 Nov 1997.*

ROBERT TRIGG, 47, SNUGGLED UP TO HIS girlfriend and accidentally killed her. The ex-chef, who weighed 182lb (82kg), had recently moved in with Susan Nicholson, 52, in Worthing, West Sussex. In April 2011, she suggested they slept on the sofa. In the morning, Trigg woke up on top of her and found her dead. At the inquest, the coroner said: "There is no evidence whatsoever that this was part of an altercation." Verdict: accident. *Sun, 12 Dec 2011.*

 A MAN WHO KILLED HIS MOTHER WITH two wooden stakes through her heart told police he thought she was a witch. The 48-year-old also handcuffed her and filled her mouth with sealing foam. He said he had saved his 70-year-old mother from eternal damnation and that she would now go to Heaven. Despite also telling police there were aliens in the flat he shared with her in Blagoveshchensk, Russia, officials said he was not mentally ill – perhaps setting a new frontier for the definition of sanity. *Sun, 18 June 2011.*

 MATTHEW HOFFMAN, 30, AN UNEMPLOYED tree trimmer from Mount Vernon, Ohio, is serving a life sentence for holding a 13-year-old girl hostage after killing her brother Kody Maynard, 11, her mother Tina Hermann, and her mother's friend Stephanie Sprang and stuffing their dismembered bodies in a hollow tree. Hoffman had an obsession with trees and leaves. His living room was stuffed with leaves, the bathroom was lined with more than 100 bags of leaves, and the captive teenager was kept bound hand and foot on a bed of leaves in the basement. His freezer contained only a couple of red popsicles and two dead squirrels. *ABC News, 10 Feb 2011.*

CHAPTER 14

Till Death Us Do Part

Even if marriage isn't always for life these days,
there are still some couples so devoted that they
literally can't live without each other...

A DEVOTED COUPLE, MARRIED FOR 44 YEARS, died within seconds of each other at their home in Huyton, Merseyside. Margaret Connell, 63, collapsed after seeing her husband Pat, 66, suffer a heart attack. They were childhood sweethearts and left 11 children and 26 grandchildren. *Times, 10 Aug 1996.*

A COUPLE MARRIED FOR 56 years died within a minute of each other. Donald Dix, 85, a retired steelworker, collapsed at home in Cardiff and his wife Rosemary dialled 999 for an ambulance. Mrs Dix, 76, stayed at home to call their two daughters with the bad news as her husband was driven off – but she was found dead with the phone still off the receiver. Mr Dix died in the ambulance on the way to hospital at almost exactly the same time Mrs Dix died. "They didn't know how to live without each other," said their daughter Jacqueline. The couple met at a dance in Nottingham, married in 1956, and were buried together. *D.Telegraph, D.Mail, 3 Feb 2011.*

ANOTHER DEVOTED COUPLE WHO WERE inseparable for more than 70 years died on the same day. Bert and Doreen Swan met in Birmingham in the late 1930s, married in 1941, and had three sons. Mrs Swan, 91, died at the nursing home in Marlborough where they both lived at 11.30am while Mr Swan, 93, who was not told of his wife's death, died in hospital of a chest infection at 10.30 that night. He had been a pioneering metallurgist. The couple retired in the 1980s and spent their time ballroom dancing and tandem riding. *D.Express, D.Mirror, 14 Jan 2011.*

IN OCTOBER 2008 ROBIN ROTHWELL was travelling to visit his 90-year-old father George in a nursing home when he

got a call saying he had died of pneumonia. Then his phone rang again, with the news that his mother Kate, 89, had been found dead at the couple's home in Torbay, Devon. Neither knew the other had died. Another couple died within hours of each other the following month, after being married for 60 years. Farmer Austin Debenham and his wife Jean were in different hospitals. Mr Debenham, 82, died of bronchial pneumonia at 11pm on 7 November. Mrs Debenham, 79, who had a heart operation, passed away at 2am that night, not knowing her husband had died. *Sun, 2 Oct, 14 Nov 2008.*

FRANK KEMP, 79, FATHER OF MARTIN AND Gary Kemp who found fame in the Eighties band Spandau Ballet, died of a heart attack in Bournemouth Hospital in January 2009. His wife Eileen, 77, who was in the same hospital after a heart bypass, died 48 hours later "of a broken heart". They had been married for 55 years. Kevin and Liz O'Connor had been married for 35 years. Mr O'Connor, a 61-year-old store manager, had a fatal heart attack near his home Stalybridge, Greater Manchester, in February 2009 after popping out to the corner shop. His wife, 58, collapsed with breathing difficulties after hearing the news and died later that day in hospital. *D.Mirror, 17 Jan; Sun, 6 Feb 2009.*

RONNIE AND CONNIE PILLING OF Emley, West Yorkshire, were married for 67 years. Mr Pilling, 86, died of pneumonia on 16 May 2009 with his wife at his bedside. She died at home the next morning of a suspected blood clot. Olga Whitfield, 61, had a heart attack at 10pm on 18 October 2009. Her husband Stewart Whitfield, 56, dialled for an ambulance but also suffered cardiac failure. Shortly afterwards, paramedics found them both dead at their home in West Boldon, South Tyneside. Fred Launder, 95, and his wife

Dorothy, 93, died at home in Newport, Isle of Wight, on the same day in December 2009 after 69 years of marriage. *D.Mirror, 18 May, 9 Dec; D.Mail, 20 Oct 2009.*

A WIDOW DIED AT THE EXACT MOMENT THE funeral began for her husband of nearly 70 years. Irene Edwards, 88, was in hospital for a broken hip and the night before the service she checked: "It's 11 o'clock, isn't it?" She died at exactly that time the next day as her beloved husband Fred, 96, of Stourport, Worcestershire, was laid to rest. *Sun, 15 Feb 2010.*

PLYMOUTH COUPLE PAT AND PERCY ROBERTS – married for 61 years – died within hours of each other on 15 January 1998. Percy, 85, who married Pat in May 1940 after a four-year courtship, had been going to see her in hospital, where she was being treated after a stroke; but he had a fatal heart attack at 4pm. Pat, 81, died peacefully in her sleep just hours later. Neither was aware of the other's passing. *Western Morning News, 30 Jan 1998.*

FLORIDA COUPLE MIRIAM AND BILL CASWELL, 87 and 83 respectively, died within 90 minutes of each other in March 2008 after 57 years of marriage. About a week later, devoted Pam Clayden, 77, and husband Eddie, 78, died within hours of each other in Kesgrave, Suffolk, after 54 years of marriage. *MX News (Brisbane), 6 Mar; Sun, 17 Mar 2008.*

Crushed

An avalanche of peanuts, a fall of killer vegetables
and the obsessive hoarders buried in their own
collections of rubbish...

WILLIE MURPHY, 61, AN EMPLOYEE OF the Golden Peanut Company in Donalsonville, Georgia, was killed in April 1993 when he was crushed under an avalanche of peanuts. The following July, a 23-year-old sweet factory worker in Marseilles, France, was crushed to death when a bin filled with 5,000lb (2,270kg) of marshmallows fell on him. *USA Today, 5 April; Daily Record, 15 July 1993.*

 WALTER FRYERS, A HEART BYPASS PATIENT, was crushed to death when a 1.5-ton tree branch fell on him during a fundraising trek for the hospital that had saved his life. Fryers, 54, died instantly and four others, including his wife, were seriously hurt when the 50ft (15m) branch broke away from the 160-year-old beech tree. There was not a breath of wind. Fifty members of the newly formed Take Heart Club were on a three-mile (5km) trek along a leafy lane in Aberford, West Yorkshire, in September 1995 to raise cash for the heart unit at Leeds General Infirmary. *D.Post, 9 Feb 1996.*

CHILDREN'S ENTERTAINER MARLON PISTOL was killed when a 20ft (6m) balloon elephant used in his act inflated in the back of his car on a California highway. *The People, 26 Oct 1997.*

THREE DAYS AFTER SHEILA KAY ROSS, 47, was reported missing in Arizona, her body was found in a delivery truck in Des Moines, Iowa, after she was crushed to death by falling lettuce. The vegetables were destroyed (as a deterrent to other vegetables?). About a week earlier, two people died and another two – all members of the same family – were injured when a truck crashed into their car on a coast road in Pontevedra, northwest Spain. Apparently, the truck driver carried out "an unusual manœuvre" while driving round a bend and his load – 20 tons of mussels – tipped onto the car. *Irish Independent, D.Record, 1 Feb; Metro Directe (Spain), 24 Jan 2007.*

 A MONTH-OLD BOY WAS KILLED WHEN HIS obese babysitter collapsed and died on top of him. Michael Baldwin III was found smothered on a sofa under 210lb (95kg) Teresa Coffey, 39. It was thought she had suffered a heart attack. The boy's father, Michael Baldwin II – a television newscaster in Long Island, New York – rushed home after Ms Coffey failed to answer his calls. At first he couldn't find his son, but then realised he was under the babysitter. A similar tragedy unfolded later the same month, also in eastern US. Allen McNeil Jr, 53, and his three-year-old son were found dead in their New Jersey home after he apparently fell on top of the infant and smothered him while having a heart attack. *Sunday Mirror, 4 Sept; Sun, 5 Sept; MX News (Brisbane), 28 Sept 2011.*

 ALLY McCRAE, 23, A CAGE FIGHTER AND expert at Thai boxing and jiu-jitsu from Kilmarnock nicknamed "McCrazy", was crushed to death by a dead cow at an abattoir in Paisley, Renfrewshire, where he worked. It is thought the one-ton carcase slipped from a hook as it was being moved along a conveyor belt. *Sun, 19 Nov 2011.*

 A COLLECTOR WHOSE HOUSE WAS SO full of junk he couldn't use the front door died after becoming struck trying to climb through an upstairs window. David Ellis, in his 60s, was found by firefighters with his legs sticking out of the window at his home in Handsworth, Birmingham. *Sunday Times, 2 Feb 1997.*

MARIE ROSE, 59, AN OBSESSIVE HOARDER living in Shelton, Washington, was reported missing by her husband, Gerald, on 5 January 2006. Police took 10 hours to find her body under a pile of junk and clothes in her home, where she had suffocated to death. "This is without a doubt the most cluttered residence I've ever been to," said Shelton Police Chief Terry Davenport. "Officers were having to climb over the top on their hands and knees, in some areas their heads were touching the ceiling while they were standing on top of piles of debris." Mr Rose said his wife had health problems and may have been looking for the phone when she died. The house contained several tons of clothing, dishes, books and boxes. *[AP] 11 Jan; Calgary Herald, 22 Jan 2006.*

 GORDON STEWART, 74, IS BELIEVED TO HAVE died of thirst after becoming lost in an intricate network of tunnels built through mountains of stinking rubbish that he had accumulated for at least a decade. The pony-tailed loner was often seen riding his bike round the streets bringing back cardboard boxes and bags full of rubbish to his two-storey semi-detached house in Broughton, Buckinghamshire. Neighbours had become concerned that they had not seen him for several days and raised the alarm on 2 January 2009. Police called in a diving team equipped with breathing apparatus because the smell from the rubbish was so overpowering. They discovered a confusing system of passageways built from discarded carrier bags, boxes, old furniture and other assorted junk around the interior of the building, with Mr Stewart entombed inside. A 1950s car in the garage had been left untouched for years as garbage built up around it. Mr Stewart had once worked as a joiner and one of his earliest jobs saw him making the wooden parts for Morris Minor 1000s. He had no known close relatives. *Manchester Eve. News, 7 Jan; Scotsman, Sun, 8 Jan 2009.*

A SIMILAR DEATH BEFELL JOAN CUNNANE, 77, around Boxing Day 2008. The retired British Telecom operator and devout Roman Catholic had bought a bungalow in Heaton Mersey, near Stockport, Greater Manchester, 16 years earlier and had been hoarding possessions ever since. The shopaholic hoarded brand-new umbrellas, candles, ornaments, trinkets, clothes (including 300 scarves) and electrical goods as well as piles of videotapes. She rarely used, or even opened, her purchases. They were neatly arranged in huge precarious piles, but took up so much space that she had only a 2ft (60cm) wide path to get around. Neighbours became concerned when they didn't see her for a few days while her Rover car remained parked outside her bungalow. She was reported missing on 6 January 2009 after failing to attend a hospital appointment.

Police with sniffer dogs went to her bungalow but failed to find her. An expert search team then sifted through her stuff, and after *two days* her body was found buried under a 3ft (90cm) pile of suitcases in a back bedroom where she had apparently gone in search of a favourite item and had died of dehydration after being trapped. Even her car was full of shopping, including dusters, a teddy bear, garden shears, bracelets, a plastic Tupperware box full of mini chocolate bars and cans of soda. "I don't know how she saw out the back of it because it was so full of stuff," said a neighbour. "Once she asked me to help her take the stuff out of the car [so that it could get an MOT]. It took us four hours." Ms Cunnane refused an offer to have the leaves swept from around her bungalow, saying they protected the pipes from frost. It was as if she couldn't part with anything. *D.Mail, D.Mirror, Metro, 9 Jan 2009.*

 A FOUR-MONTH SEARCH FOR A MISSING woman ended when she was found at home buried under piles of rubbish. The body of Billie Jean James, 67, was eventually found by her husband, who had been living in the same bungalow in Las Vegas, Nevada. He had been clearing out a back room in August 2010 when he spotted one of her feet. Police had searched the place three times using sniffer dogs, but they were unable to find the body of the compulsive hoarder amid floor-to-ceiling piles of clothes, rubbish, empty food boxes and other goods. It was thought rotting food and other pungent smells prevented the dogs from working properly. Small pathways had been cleared to allow the couple to move around. Mr James, 68, reported his wife missing the previous April. He feared she might have suffered a stroke and become disoriented. *Telegraph.co.uk, 29 Aug; D.Mail, 30 Aug 2010.*

 A GERMAN COUPLE IN THEIR 50s TOOK THEIR old car to a scrapyard. They parked, completed the paperwork, but got back in the car to shelter from a sudden squall of rain. "The driver of the crane was told to process their car," said a police investigator. "He did so without realising the couple were sitting inside again." The car was grabbed by the crane's steel claws and dropped in the crusher, which normally reduces cars to a small cube. It was stopped when the crane driver heard the woman's screams, but it was too late to save her husband. The crane driver was hospitalised for shock, but was expected to be charged with "negligent manslaughter". *D.Mail, 14 April 1997.*

All in the Mind

Depressed, delusional or just plain bonkers: unusual
states of mind lead to unusual deaths...

WHEN SHARON R LOPATKA LEFT HER home in Hampstead, Maryland, on 13 October 1996, she wrote a note for her husband saying she was going to visit friends in Georgia and would not be coming back. "If my body is never retrieved, don't worry, know that I am at peace," she wrote. She also asked him not to go after her attacker. In the event, Lopatka took a 300-mile (480km) bus ride to North Carolina, where she expected to be sexually tortured and killed by a man with whom she had corresponded over the Internet.

Apparently, she got her wish. Her body was found in a shallow grave in late October behind a mobile home in Collettsville. The autopsy showed she had been strangled about 16 October. The home's owner, Robert Glass, was charged with first-degree murder. Messages from Glass, recovered from Lopatka's home computer, indicated that she travelled to North Carolina knowing what awaited her. Lopatka, 35, operated three websites. One offered to write classified advertisements, while the other two, advertising psychic hotlines, were entitled 'Psychics Know All' and 'Dionne Enterprises'. A friend described her as happily married and sensible. Glass, 45, a father of three who separated from his wife earlier in the year, worked as a computer programmer for the county for nearly 16 years. The two first came into contact over the Internet.

Lopatka's husband reported her missing on 20 October and police discovered the email messages from Glass despite his attempt to have her erase the files. Messages from 'Slowhand' – Glass's apparent Internet alias – "described in detail how he was going to sexually torture… and ultimately kill her," according to an affidavit. *[AP] 29 Oct 1996.*

PATRICIA HALL, 72, A FORMER SECRETARY from Eastbourne, East Sussex, "drowned" by drinking water, but may have been unable to stop, an inquest was told in September 2003. She had been diagnosed with schizophrenia in 1986. Pathologist Christopher

Moffatt said that the level of sodium in the blood had dropped so much that she developed water on the lungs, leading to pulmonary œdema. He said: "A normal lung weighs between 300 and 400 grams [11oz and 14oz]. Mrs Hall's right lung weighed 1.073 grams [38oz] and her left, 864 grams [30oz]. She drank a lot of liquid. We are talking gallons and gallons."

Shaun McNamara, 35, was found dead on his bathroom floor in Yorkshire in September 2007, his brain swollen due to water intoxication. At an inquest in York the following February, the coroner said there was nothing to suggest Mr McNamara, who had a history of depression, tried to kill himself. The death was ruled an accident.

Hours after being sent home from a mental hospital in Scarborough, North Yorkshire, depressed Gilly Strawman, 37, drank six litres (11 pints) of water in an hour and then drank some more from a tap – flooding her lungs and brain. She was rushed to hospital but died from water intoxication a few days later. In April 2008, the verdict was accident contributed to by neglect.

Andrew Thornton, 44, a warehouse worker from Bradford, West Yorkshire, suffered from gingivitis for 20 years and shunned painkillers, instead drinking water to numb his gums. On 5 December 2007 he drank more than 17 pints (9.6 litres) in just eight hours, dangerously lowering sodium levels in his body. Even when he started vomiting, he still quaffed more. He collapsed and was taken to hospital, where medics initially thought he was drunk because he was staggering and slurring his words. He died from a heart attack the next day. *Times, 3 Sept 2003; Metro, 1 Feb, 8 July; Sun, 1 Feb, 30 April, 8 July 2008.*

JANE LINTON, 56, PLUNGED THREE STOREYS to her death from her bedroom window in Redcliffe Gardens, south-west London, on 16 January 2008. In the days before her death, she had been acting "very strangely" and claimed police were in the house and "out

to get her', according to her friend of 20 years, Rhian Bradley. Six months earlier, she had been bitten by a tick while working on land around a house in France owned by Miss Bradley. She returned to London in December to seek medical help for debilitating joint pains that left her walking on crutches. Her GP suspected Lyme disease, a tick-borne illness that can cause psychosis and delusions, and sent her for tests. Her mental state rapidly deteriorated.

Miss Bradley, who lived with Miss Linton, said her friend became exhausted from lack of sleep and started suffering from delusions. "Jan began to have doubts and questioned the whole meaning of her life," she said. Coroner Dr Paul Knapman said Miss Linton was "clearly not herself" at the time of her death and her behaviour was "totally out of character". He recorded a verdict of death by misadventure. Lyme disease is on the increase in the UK due to warmer, wetter weather. In 2006, there were 768 reported cases, compared with 292 in 2003. *(London) Eve. Standard, 10 April; D.Mail, 11 April 2008.*

CHAPTER 17

Boiling Point

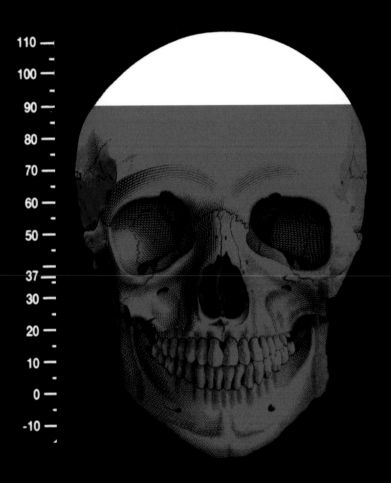

Whether it's a slow-burning resentment nurtured for
years or an explosion of sudden rage, when people
see red the consequences can be fatal...

JOSEPH FALLAR SR, 61, WAS ARRESTED ON 15 August 1992 at his house in Harrison City, Pennsylvania, for the murder of his wife Florene, 50, whom he had stabbed 219 times. "He told me he killed his wife," said Patrolman John Simcoviak. "He said she would stack the refrigerator full of vegetables, hiding the milk, and he wasn't going to take that any more." *[AP] 17 Aug 1992.*

BRAZILIAN PSYCHIATRIST OSCAR DOMINGUEZ, 45, shot dead a woman patient in his São Paulo office as she told him about her sex life. "I couldn't take those nut-cases any more," he told a court, where he faced a 25-year sentence. *D.Star, 27 Nov 1992.*

YIANNIS KARAYANNOPOULOS, 87, A farmer in Oropedio, near Grevena in northern Greece, believed that his cat had been stolen by his neighbour, Thomas Koletsos, so he shot him dead as he left for work on 10 May 1995. Mr Koletsos's wife Chrysanthi heard the shot, rushed out and was shot dead in turn. Karayannopoulos then turned the gun on himself. The cat returned later in the day. *[AP] 12 May 1995.*

HASIEM ZAYED, 59, A SHORT-ORDER COOK, and waitress Helen Menicou, 47, had worked together et the Pine Crest Diner in San Francisco for 22 fractious years. On 23 July 1997, she publicly scolded him for making poached eggs for a customer when it was not on the menu. This was the last straw: the next morning he came to work and shot her dead. *[AP] 25 July 1997.*

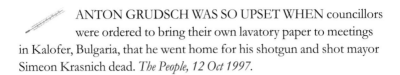

ANTON GRUDSCH WAS SO UPSET WHEN councillors were ordered to bring their own lavatory paper to meetings in Kalofer, Bulgaria, that he went home for his shotgun and shot mayor Simeon Krasnich dead. *The People, 12 Oct 1997.*

A ROMANIAN WOMAN, FLORICA IFRIMIE, hanged herself before her wedding because she could not agree with her bridegroom over the menu for the wedding feast. *National (Romania), 14 Nov 1997.*

SEYYED HASHEM AHMAD, 43, AN Egyptian house painter, pushed a 65-year-old woman, Ensaf Mohmamad [sic] Selim, to her death from the roof of a three-storey building in Suez following a dispute over who should be allowed to hang out their washing first. *Halifax Eve. Courier, 4 Nov 1997.*

A SPANIARD CONFESSED TO KILLING ANOTHER man for taking a sip of his drink by mistake in a bar. Barcelona prosecutors sought a 12-year jail sentence for Dino Marcelo Miller, 31. *Newcastle Journal, 1 June 2000.*

A MAN WHO LOST AN EARLY-MORNING Bible-quoting contest killed the man who beat him. Gabel Taylor, 38, was shot once in the face outside his apartment in Dadeville, Alabama, on 18 July 1996. Police were searching for the suspect, who was thought to have left Dadeville. Taylor, a preacher's brother, and the suspect were comparing their Bible knowledge outside an apartment complex, each quoting different versions of the same passage. The

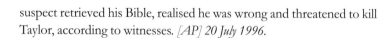

suspect retrieved his Bible, realised he was wrong and threatened to kill Taylor, according to witnesses. *[AP] 20 July 1996.*

EUGENE AND PEARLE COGSWELL HAD been happily married for 20 years. In August 2002 she baked a blueberry pie and said she planned to give it to a relative. He threw a glass of wine in her face; she rang the Maine police; he shot her and then killed himself. *Independent on Sunday, 18 Aug 2002.*

A PRISONER WAS KILLED AFTER HIS SNORING drove a cellmate into a violent rage. Thomas Brady, 22, was stabbed with a sharpened table knife as he slept in his cell in Dublin's Mountjoy prison on Easter Sunday 2000. He was rushed to hospital but couldn't be saved. *Tanzania Guardian, 26 April 2000.*

A MAN WAS SHOT DEAD AT A LATVIAN cinema on 19 February 2011 after eating his popcorn too loudly during the movie *Black Swan*, starring Natalie Portman. The dispute broke out at Riga's Forum Cinemas complex towards the end of the film, and lawyer Nikolajs Zikovs, 27, shot Aigars Egle, 42, as the credits rolled. *telegraph. co.uk, 21 Feb; Sydney Morning Herald, 24 Feb 2011.*

A GLOOMY ANGLER STABBED HIS BEST FRIEND to death for being too happy after a drink and drugs binge. Craig Walter, 34, knifed 48-year-old Maurice Wilson 17 times after he said: "I love life". The pair had smoked 15 joints by a canal in east London before the row. Walter, of the Isle of Dogs, was jailed for life. *Sun, 17 Sept 2005.*

Accidents Will Happen

Freak accidents can result in the unlikeliest deaths –
from the woman with a toilet brush stuck in her bum
to the chef impaled by flying spaghetti...

EAGER TO TRY ON A £750 TOUPEE, SHOP manager Claude Jules, 53, of Abbeville, France, stopped his car, dabbed on special glue and applied the wig. Then he lit a cigarette. The glue fumes ignited and the car exploded, killing him instantly. *(Scottish) Daily Record, 2 Jan 1992.*

KEN CHARLES BARGER, 47, ACCIDENTALLY shot himself to death in Newton, North Carolina, in December 1992. Awakening to the sound of a ringing telephone beside his bed, he reached for the phone but grabbed instead a Smith & Wesson .38 Special, which discharged when he drew it to his ear. *Hickory Daily Record, 21 Dec 1992.*

EFRAIN GONZALES, 43, WAS TOSSING TRIMMINGS from a lemon orchard into a wood chipper on Reimen's Ranch in Ventura County, California, on 22 April 1999 when he got pulled into the machine's blades and reduced to pulp. The machine was capable of grinding trees up to 16in (40cm) in diameter. There was a safety lever, but Gonzales apparently couldn't reach it in time. It was thought one of his long sleeves got snagged in the machine. Two deaths in wood chippers occurred in Maine in 2000: Michele Carrier, 51, in Skowhegan (March) and Adam Evangelista, 20, in Solon (September). *Los Angeles Times, 23 April 1999; Lewiston (ME) Sun Journal, 3 Mar, 23 Sept 2000.*

MARK ROCKINGHAM, 12, DIED ON 30 March 1997 when he fell on a knife that had been stacked with its blade pointing upwards in the cutlery basket of an open dishwasher. He is believed to have reached into a cupboard at his home in Kettering, Northamptonshire, when he lost his balance and fell forwards across the front of the machine. The knife sliced through an artery in his chest and he died in hospital.

The same fate befell a man in his mid 50s on 24 April 2001, when sharp objects in his mother's dishwasher's cutlery rack fatally pierced his chest. The man was in Vernon, near Vancouver, visiting his mother's home after the death of his father. He was standing near the appliance when he apparently began to feel unwell and collapsed on top of the open door. *Guardian, D.Telegraph, D.Mirror, 2 April 1997; Vancouver Sun, 28 April 2001.*

JOAN DAVIES, 72, OF LITTLE CHALFONT, Buckinghamshire, died after slipping in her bathroom and impaling herself on the lavatory brush. It went straight through her eyes and 7in (17cm) into her brain. It is not known if she died instantly. Her body was found after worried neighbours telephoned police. *D.Record, 15 July 1995.*

CINDY CORTON, 35, OF SLEAFORD, Lincolnshire, had a 6in (15cm) long toilet brush handle embedded in her buttock after a drunken fall in a friend's bathroom in 2005. She went to hospital but was sent home with painkillers despite showing medics the wound in her bottom. Four days later she was in such pain that she went for X-rays, but nothing was found. It was two years of constant pain before she was able to convince doctors that the thin serrated plastic handle was stuck in her arse cheek. By then it had become much more dangerous because it was embedded in her pelvis. After two unsuccessful operations in 2007, Mrs Curton agreed to undergo further surgery in June 2009, but died from massive blood loss. Her husband was suing United Lincolnshire Hospitals Trust. *Sun, 18 May 2010.*

TAXIDERMIST ROELF UYS WAS celebrating his 33rd birthday in the bush in South Africa's Northern Province in 1996 when a hunter saw his hat bobbing in the long grass and, mistaking it for a pheasant, shot him dead.

A similar fate befell Greek hunter Nicholas Kavalakis, 79. Since he was a young man, he had made a living by luring wolves for hunting through expertly imitating their cries. On 10 August 2000, Abdi Mehmetoglou, 57, and two companions went hunting in Sufli, Thrace, near the Greek-Turkish border, allowing wolf-cryer Kavalakis to stalk ahead.

Unaware that he had crouched in dense bushes to make his calls, and thinking they had come upon a real wolf, the three men opened fire into the foliage. Kavalakis was shot dead. The three hunters were jailed pending charges of negligence leading to manslaughter and illegal hunting. Up to 1,000 wolves live wild in Greece, but hunting them had been banned since 1993. *D. Telegraph, 6 July 1996, 12 Aug 2000; Metro, 11 Aug 2000.*

RETIRED TEACHER ANN NEWTON, 58, DROWNED in her shallow pond in Penshaw, near Sunderland, on 3 February 2011, after being pinned underwater by a garden ornament. She was filling a bird feeder when she slipped on wet grass. As she fell, her blouse snagged the carved tree trunk, which toppled and trapped her face-down under the 18in (46cm)-deep water. Her devastated partner, Norman Lunn, found her after returning from a walk. *Sunderland Echo, 12 May; Sun, 13 May 2011.*

"THIS IS A TRAGICALLY BIZARRE CASE," ruled the State Appeals Court in Chicago, "and case law involving flying bodies is sparse. Nevertheless, the facts are clear. In 2008, 18-year-old Hiroyuki Joho was hurrying in pouring rain across the tracks, with an umbrella over his head, to catch an inbound train at Edgebrook Metra station in Chicago, when he was struck by a southbound Amtrak train travelling at more than 70mph [113km/h]. A large portion of his body was thrown 100ft [30m] onto the southbound platform, where it struck Gayane Zokhrabov, then aged 58, who was waiting to catch the 8.17 to work. She was knocked to the ground by Joho's corpse, her leg and wrist were broken, and she sued Joho's estate for negligence by allowing his body to injure her." After the appeals court ruled in favour of Ms Zokhrabov, her lawyer Leslie Rosen told reporters: "While the circumstances of this case are gory and creepy, it should be treated like a regular negligence case. If you do something as stupid as this guy did, you have to be responsible for what comes from it, even if you're dead." *Chicago Tribune, Los Angeles Times, dailymail.co.uk, 29 Dec 2011.*

JEREMY T BRENNO, 16, SLAMMED HIS No. 3-wood golf club against a bench after making a bad shot at the Kingsboro Golf Club in Gloversville, New York. He bled to death after the club's broken shaft snapped back and pierced his pulmonary vein. *[AP] 12 July 1994.*

ARAZ SALEH, 23, DIED AFTER FALLING off a bucket of mayonnaise and stabbing himself in the heart with an electric drill. He had one foot on the industrial-sized bucket and one on a table while fixing metal panels to the side of a friend's fast food kiosk in Gloucester Green, Oxford, in November 2010. He lost his footing and as he fell his left shoulder hit a wall, driving the power tool into his chest. "Then I saw blood gushing out," said his friend, Salam Kiras. "It was an incredibly unusual injury," a policewoman told the inquest in Oxford. *dailymail.co.uk, D.Mirror, 9 Feb 2012.*

JUST BEFORE CHRISTMAS 1993, DIMITRU Dumitrazcu, a farmer from Slatiora in Romania, was distilling brandy in his cellar when he was overcome by the fumes and fell into the barrel. He was dead when his wife found him. *Delict Magazin (Romania), April 1994.*

A 17-YEAR-OLD HONG KONG GIRL WAS killed when a tethered balloon she was strapped to broke free and drifted 25 miles (40km) before bursting and throwing her to the ground. The body of the teenager, part of a tour group visiting a movie theme park in Panyu, southern China, was found five hours after the balloon took off. Why she was strapped to the balloon is not explained. *Western Morning News, 21 Mar 1996.*

A 27-YEAR-OLD MAN, NAMED ON A KITE website as Marcos, was killed on 24 July after being swept 50ft (15m) into the air by his power kite and plunging to the ground. He was with his family and friends when he was caught by a gust of wind and carried away. It is not clear if he let go of the kite, which had a 19ft (5.8m) wingspan, or was flung back to the ground as he held on at Dunstable Downs in Bedfordshire. He broke his arm, pelvis and both legs, and was pronounced dead at the scene from a suspected heart attack. *D.Mail, 26 July 2011.*

CHEF JUAN RUIZ WAS STABBED THROUGH the heart with uncooked spaghetti strands when 150mph (240km/h) winds hit his restaurant in Mexico City. Two months later, a young employee of the Bennett Food Factory in the Bronx, New York, died instantly when he fell head-first into an industrial dough-mixer making macaroni and was impaled by the mixing blades. *The People, 28 Aug; NY Post, 27 Oct 1994.*

A GERMAN TOURIST WAS KILLED WHEN a beach umbrella uprooted by a freak tornado struck him on the head at the Bulgarian resort of Albena. (We recall that other lethal Bulgarian umbrella, used to assassinate the dissident Georgi Markov in London in 1978.) *D.Mirror, 23 July 1996.*

A 32-YEAR-OLD MAN FELL 3,000ft (914m) to his death after his electric wheelchair suddenly shot forward into a ravine near Trento, Italy. *Sun, 17 Aug 2011.*

KARATE BROWN BELT AND THAI BOXING enthusiast Scott Kell, 23, lost his balance doing high kicks and plunged to his death through an open window on the 10th floor of a tower block in Salford, Manchester, on 6 July 1993. *D.Mail, 17 Nov 1994.*

A MAN DROWNED ON 11 MARCH AFTER falling from a flimsy stepladder and landing head-first in a water butt at his home in Fleet in Lincolnshire. Retired printer Arthur Sexton, 80, was found with his legs poking out of the 4ft (1.2m) deep butt by neighbour Ian Bond after his wife raised the alarm. He was wedged in so tight he was unable to pull himself free. "I had to shake him out he was in so tight," said Mr Bond. *D.Mail, Metro, D.Mirror, 21 April 2011.*

NEIL MICKLEWRIGHT, 19, DIED AFTER accidentally stabbing himself in the eye with a screwdriver while breaking into a church safe in Oldbury, West Midlands. He was found writhing in agony by paramedics. *D.Record, 13 May 2000.*

A CHINESE TRAIN GUARD DIED AFTER HE urinated on goods in a cargo wagon and set off a chemical reaction that produced toxic hydrogen phosphide gas. He was found unconscious when the train arrived in the northern port city of Tianjin. *[AFP] 18 April 1996.*

CHAPTER 19

Death by Reptile

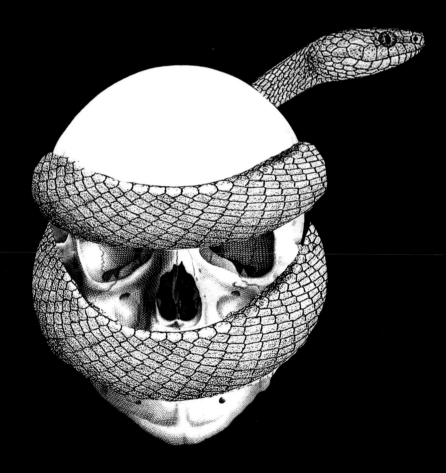

Snakes, crocodiles, alligators, Komodo dragons:
reptiles have a fearsome reputation - and in these
cases it appears to be deserved...

FOUR BOYS IN THE WESTERN ALGERIAN city of Maghnia, aged from eight to 15, died shortly after eating soup. Their mother had inadvertently brought home a poisonous snake hidden in vegetables which she put in the family fridge. The snake, seeking warmth, slithered into a soup pot and discharged its venom into the soup. *[AFP] 4 May 1992.*

WHEN A SAUDI WOMAN ARRIVED IN THE eastern city of Dammam to visit her daughter and her new-born child, she complained of "strange movements" down her back during the journey from the south. Her daughter pulled back her dress to investigate and received a fatal bite from a viper. *[AFP] 16 Oct 1996.*

A SNAKE MANAGED TO ESCAPE FROM the claws of an eagle and fell into a car near Khaf in the Iranian province of Khorassan, where it bit four passengers in June 2002. Two were killed instantly and two others injured and taken to the local hospital. Khaf is 160 miles (258km) south east of the provincial capital of Mashhad. *Islamic Republic News Agency (IRNA), 30 June 2002.*

ON 17 NOVEMBER 2002, A GROUP OF boys went to pick mangoes in an old orchard at Lamontville, near Durban in South Africa. One 10-year-old remained on the ground while the others climbed mango trees and threw the fruit down to him. When he ventured into tall grass to fetch some that had rolled there, he was attacked by an enormous African rock python. The others watched in horror as the snake coiled itself around him, constricted him until he passed out, and swallowed him head-first. Terrified, they remained up the trees for

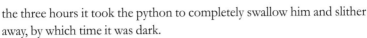

the three hours it took the python to completely swallow him and slither away, by which time it was dark.

Khaye Buthelezi, 11, ran home and told his mother what had happened. Judging by marks left in the sand, Craig Smith, co-owner of the Fitzsimmons Snake Park in Durban, said the snake must have been between 5.5m and 6m (18–20ft) long. Khaye's description of the snake's markings and killing technique convinced Smith that the boy had, indeed, been swallowed. "He didn't cry or scream," said Khaye, "and neither did the rest of us – we didn't want the snake to come and take us as well." There were signs of a struggle in the grass and the snake left tracks on its way to a nearby stream. The tracks ended at the waterside. Smith said it could take up to two months before the snake hunted again.

African rock pythons can grow up to 8.5 metres (28ft) and usually feed on monkeys, pigs, deer, small apes and birds. Smith said this particular snake had probably just awoken from its winter hibernation and was extremely hungry when the boy wandered into its path. *News 24.com (South Africa), 20+21 Nov; Sydney Morning Herald, 22 Nov; Sunday Telegraph, 24 Nov; D.Mail, 25 Nov 2002.*

BASANTI TRIPURA, 38, WAS COLLECTING fruit with a friend in a forest in the Rangamati district of Bangladesh on 18 November 2003 when she was attacked by a 10ft (3m) python. By the time her companion had raised the alarm and rescuers had arrived on the scene, the snake had crushed her in its coils and swallowed her head-first up to the waist. Villagers retrieved her body after beating the snake to death with iron rods and sticks and cutting it open. Rangamati is a region of forests and rugged hills, 135 miles (217km) southeast of the capital Dhaka. *[R] 21 Nov; D.Mirror, 22 Nov 2003.*

MANSUR, AN EIGHT- (OR NINE-) YEAR-OLD boy, was mauled to death by a Komodo dragon in eastern Indonesia on 2 June 2007. He was with his uncle mending fishing nets (or relieving himself in a bush) on Komodo Island – one of the largest in the Komodo national park – when the dragon attacked him. It clawed his right leg, bit him in the stomach with its serrated teeth and shook him in an attempt to break his neck. His uncle and other men pelted the creature with rocks until it released the boy, who was unconscious and bleeding heavily. Before a boat could be arranged to take him to a doctor, he had died of his injuries. Even if he had survived the initial attack, say experts, he would have been killed by blood-poisoning from the bacteria in the dragon's saliva.

The park, and the western and northern coastlines of neighbouring Flores island, are the natural habitat of the dragon, the world's largest monitor lizard, which can grow up to 10ft (3m) and weigh as much as 300lb (136kg). It can live for up to 50 years, and sprint at 15mph (24km/h), and its usual prey are monkeys, wild deer and rats. There were an estimated 3,000 remaining in the park and surrounding areas.

Muhamad Anwar, 31, was picking fruit up a sugar apple tree on Komodo Island on 25 March 2009, when he fell to the ground and was mauled by a couple of komodo dragons. The man's neighbour, Theresia Tawa, said he was bleeding badly from bites to his hands, body, legs and neck. He died at a clinic on Flores.

While attacks on humans are extremely rare, a local story persists of a Swiss tourist who vanished while on an expedition to photograph the creatures in the wild in the 1990s. His binoculars and torn clothing were found in the jungle. In 1974, an elderly European tourist, Baron Rudolf von Reding Biberegg, fell and injured his knee on a hiking trip on Komodo Island. His guide returned to a village to seek help. All the search party found was the man's hat, camera and a bloodstained shoe.
[AFP] 4 June; D.Mail, 5 June 2007; [AP] 25 Mar 2009.

A MAN IN THAILAND WAS FOUND DEAD WITH A cobra carcass in his hands and a condom on his penis. The body of Wiroj Banlen, 40, was discovered on the side of a dirt road near the village of Lamsai in Ayutthaya province. There were several snake-bites on his right leg and his cheeks; the dead cobra found clenched in his hands had also been bitten several times. Snake remnants were found in his teeth, suggesting he had bitten the animal. The condom contained no semen, and the police believe he was either putting on or removing his trousers when the snake struck. *Metro, 9 June 2008.*

AN INEBRIATED VISITOR TO LAKE Carpintero sanctuary near Tampico, Mexico, leaned over a rail to stroke a crocodile in August 2008, and was dragged into the water. He was then ripped to pieces by eight crocodiles and consumed in front of 50 tourists. "It's unheard of for eight crocodiles to join forces in killing a man," said fire department spokesman Ramiro Alos. "It's the most savage attack in living memory in Mexico. There are no remains and we can't identify him. He must have suffered horrifically." *Sun, 18 Aug 2008.*

AN ESCAPED CROCODILE CAUSED A PLANE crash on 25 August 2010, killing 20 people. The internal flight in the Democratic Republic of Congo got into trouble when passengers stampeded in the cabin, throwing the Czech-made, twin-engined Let L-410 Turbojet off balance, the sole survivor told investigators. The crocodile survived the crash, only to be dispatched with a blow from a machete.

Danny Philemotte, 62, the Belgian (or Dutch) pilot and owner of the plane's operator, Filair, struggled in vain with the controls, with Chris Wilson, his 39-year-old first officer, from Shurdington, Gloucestershire. The plane was on a routine flight from Kinshasa to the regional airport of Bandundu. It crashed into a house as few hundred feet from its destination. The occupants of the property were not in at the time.

A passenger had hidden the crocodile, which he planned to sell, in a big sports bag from which it escaped as the plane began its descent. The report of the incident said: "The terrified air hostess hurried towards the cockpit, followed by the passengers." The plane was then sent off-balance "despite the desperate efforts of the pilot". *D.Telegraph, D.Mail, 22 Oct 2010.*

ALLIGATORS KILLED THREE WOMEN IN Florida within a single week – after 58 years in which only 17 people had died as a result of such attacks. On 9 May 2006, Yovy Suarez Jiminez, 28, cooling her feet in a canal in Sunrise, 25 miles (40km) north of Miami, was dragged into the water. Her dismembered body was found the next day and four days later, a one-eyed alligator trapped nearby was found to have her arms in its stomach. Then Annmarie Campbell, 23, was killed while snorkelling in Lake St George, 80 miles (130km) north of Orlando; and on 14 May the dismembered body of Judy Cooper, 43, was found in a canal near Dunedin on the west coast, 20 miles (32km) north of St Petersburg.

Some experts linked the attacks to the severe drought gripping parts of the state. The low water levels in the Everglades could have been forcing the alligators into residential areas in search of food and water. May is the mating season, which makes the critters more aggressive – and demographic pressure is reducing their habitat. "As the weather heats up, the alligators' metabolism increases and they have to eat more," said Willie Puz, a spokesman for the Florida Fish and Wildlife Commission. "But that shouldn't mean increased attacks." *Independent, 13+16+20 May; Guardian, 16 May 2006.*

CHAPTER 20

Funeral Foul-ups

The phrase "It's your funeral" doesn't always apply,
as this selection of mortuary mix-ups, mistaken
identities and premature burials shows...

PHILIPPE DELMARIE, 39, FROM Thiaucourt-Régnéville in the French département of Meurthe-et-Moselle, left home in 1987 to live in the Rhône valley and progressively lost touch with his family. In February 1989, a body was fished out of the Rhône and identified as Delemarie by his boss and another man. Both Delemarie and the dead man had a scar on the lower left cheek. The body was buried in the family grave. Then in July 1989 the family took a phone call from Philippe's ex-girlfriend, who said that he was living in Sables d'Olonne in the Vendée département on the Atlantic coast. The police were trying to establish who had been buried in his place. *Le Quotidien (Réunion), 18 July 1989.*

A JAPANESE SHIPBUILDER AGED 60 came home from work in April 2000 to find his family busy making arrangements for his funeral. Police had told the family that the man had died in a car crash, after his brother-in-law wrongly identified a body. *[R] 17 April 2000.*

MOURNERS IN A MALAYSIAN VILLAGE were flabbergasted when a man they thought they had just buried walked into a prayer session after his funeral. Che Mohamad Shamsul Abdul Rahman, 22, had been missing for 10 days when the decomposed body of a drowning victim was found near his village in Selising, about 300 miles (483km) north-east of Kuala Lumpur. His father, Abdul Rahman Ibrahim, said that he identified features on the body similar to those of his son. Villagers said the "dead" man had walked in "as though nothing had happened". *[AP] 20 July 2002.*

NGUYEN VAN BINH, A 48-YEAR-OLD Vietnamese soldier, suffered head injuries fighting in Cambodia in 1978 and was left with amnesia. He wandered out of hospital in the early 1980s and got lost, then worked as a labourer. His unit, unable to find him, declared him dead in 1985. In 2001, he was adopted by a family and slowly began recovering his memory. A police officer helped him remember the name of his home village. In August 2002 he was reunited with his family in Kim Lan village outside Hanoi. *[AP] 22 Aug 2002.*

A FUNERAL IN WISCONSIN TURNED INTO a celebration when the dead man phoned home. The family of Danny Spohn had been told a train had hit him because his brother-in-law had identified the body; the grief-stricken family made the funeral arrangements and an obituary notice was published in the local paper. Danny got in touch after showing up at a friend's house and being told he was meant to be dead. His sister Debbie Mason said she couldn't believe it when he called. "We thought it was a cruel joke," she said. "There was shock and joy… We sent my brother Paul to get him. We were going to leave nothing to chance."

At the time of the report in August 2002, Danny Spohn was out of touch again. "It's just a miracle he hadn't taken off fishing," said his father. "We would have buried him." Police said they were almost certain they had now correctly identified the body found on the railway. *Ananova, 30 July; Irish Independent, 3 Aug 2002.*

A FUNERAL IN ROMANIA WAS CALLED OFF after the dead man called his family asking if they would pick him up from hospital. The body, thought to be that of 59-year-old rail accident victim Ioan Pancu, had been washed, dressed and was waiting at the family home for burial when he called his wife. "The body looks just like him," said a relative. In August 2002 police in the town of Botosani were trying to identify the body. *Sunday Times, 4 Aug 2002.*

MOURNERS SCREAMED IN HORROR AFTER Edison Vicuna turned up drunk at his own funeral in Cuenca, Ecuador. Some of them even fainted. His family and friends were mourning a body they thought was Vicuna after he went missing for three days. Jorge Matute, who had performed the post mortem examination, told the *Terra Noticias Populares* newspaper: "The body had its face disfigured after a car crash and was mistaken for Vicuna." The dead man was returned to the morgue where it was correctly identified. *Ananova, 15 Oct 2002.*

A WOMAN DIED FROM A HEART ATTACK caused by the shock of waking up at her own funeral in Kazan, Russia. As mourning relatives filed past her open coffin, Fagilyu Mukhametzyanov, 49, woke up and started screaming as she realised where she was. Her husband Fagili, 51, had been told his wife had died of a heart attack after she had collapsed at home with chest pains. "Her eyes fluttered and we immediately rushed her back to the hospital, but she only lived for another 12 minutes before she died again, this time for good," he said. "She wasn't dead when they said she was and they could have saved her." He planned to sue the hospital. *dailymail.co.uk, 23 June 2011.*

CHAPTER 21

Not OK Computer

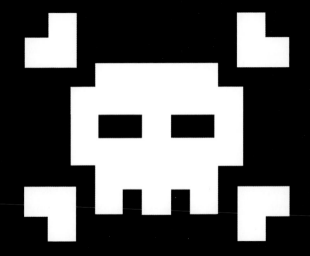

As new technologies like computers and the Internet change our lives, they also create new dangers - like death from playing video games...

A 24-YEAR-OLD UNEMPLOYED MAN, identified by police only by his last name, Kim, was found dead on 8 October 2002 in the lavatory of an Internet café in Kwangju, South Korea. He had been playing computer games non-stop for 86 hours, with no decent sleep or meals.

Eleven days later, Lien Wen-cheng, 27, was found foaming from the mouth and bleeding from the nose in the lavatory of an Internet café in Fengyuan, central Taiwan. He had been playing video games non-stop for 32 hours straight. He was rushed to hospital, but died on the way.

On 11 January 2003, a 28-year-old unnamed man was found slumped dead at a computer terminal in a game centre in Hong Kong. For the previous five hours, he had been playing the on-line game *Diablo II*. *Edinburgh Eve. News, 9 Oct; [DPA] Bangkok Post (Thailand), 20 Oct 2002, 13 Jan 2003.*

A 31-YEAR-OLD COMPUTER GAME ADDICT collapsed and died on 6 March 2004 at his screen in Chengdu in the western Chinese province of Sichuan, after playing the online game *Saga* for 20 hours, according to the *South China Morning Post*. He had been playing the game regularly at the Internet café, where an employee said he would often play for more than 10 hours a day. *The Press (Christchurch, NZ), 10 Mar 2004.*

A SOUTH KOREAN MAN DIED AFTER reportedly playing an online computer game for 50 hours with few breaks. Lee, 28, identified only by his family name, collapsed after playing the battle simulation game *Starcraft* at an Internet café in the city of Taegu. More than 15 million South Koreans, a third of the population, are registered for online gaming. Multi-player gaming is televised and professional players are treated (and paid) like sports stars. They make more than $100,000 a year. Lee had recently been fired because he kept missing work to play computer games. He started playing *Starcraft* on 3 August 2005 and only paused to go to the lavatory or for short naps. "We presume the cause of death was heart failure stemming from exhaustion," said a police official. *BBC News, 10 Aug 2005.*

A MAN AGED ABOUT 30 FROM THE southern Chinese boomtown of Guangzhou died in hospital on 15 September 2007 after playing games at an Internet café for three consecutive days. The *Beijing News* said that exhaustion was the most likely cause of death. It did not say what game he had been playing. The previous March, an obese 26-year-old Chinese man collapsed and died after spending "almost all" of the week-long New Year holiday playing games on his computer. *Metro, 1 Mar; [R] 17 Sept 2007.*

A COMPUTER-ADDICTED COUPLE FROM Suwon in South Korea let their three-month-old baby starve to death in September 2009 while raising a virtual daughter online. The jobless pair fed their premature baby powdered milk once a day and then spent 12 hours at an Internet café nurturing virtual girl Anima through their avatars on a Second Life-style game called *Prius Online*. The 45-year-old man and his wife, 25, met through a chat website. They were sentenced to two years' jail in May 2010. The wife's term was suspended because she was pregnant with a second child. *Guardian, 6 Mar; Irish Independent, 29 May 2010.*

FORTEAN TIMES WOULD LIKE TO THANK:

The many readers who, over the years, have sent in the newspaper clippings or Internet links from which the stories in this volume have been compiled.

GET INVOLVED – BECOME A **FORTEAN TIMES** CLIPSTER!

Regular clipsters have provided the lifeblood of **Fortean Times** since it began in 1973. One of the delights for the editors is receiving packets of clips from Borneo or Brazil, Saudi Arabia or Siberia. We invite you to join in the fun and send in anything weird, from trade journals, local newspapers, extracts from obscure tomes, or library newspaper archives.

To minimise the time spent on preparing clippings for a Fort Sort, we ask that you cut them out and not fold them too small. Mark each clip (on the front, where possible) with the source, date and your name, so that we can credit you in the listing when we use the material. For UK local and overseas clips, please give the town of publication. For foreign language clips, we appreciate brief translations. To avoid confusion over day and month, please write the date in this form: 10 July 2012. If you send photocopies, copy on one side of the paper only.

Mail to: **Fortean Times, PO Box 2409, London NW5 4NP, UK**
E-mail: **sieveking@forteantimes.com**
or post on the FT website at **www.forteantimes.co.uk,**
where there is a contributor's guide.